T0372344

Cambridge Elements ≡

Elements in Publishing and Book Culture
edited by
Samantha Rayner
University College London
Leah Tether
University of Bristol

OLD DELHI'S PARALLEL BOOK BAZAAR

Kanupriya Dhingra

CAMBRIDGE
UNIVERSITY PRESS

CAMBRIDGE
UNIVERSITY PRESS

Shaftesbury Road, Cambridge CB2 8EA, United Kingdom

One Liberty Plaza, 20th Floor, New York, NY 10006, USA

477 Williamstown Road, Port Melbourne, VIC 3207, Australia

314–321, 3rd Floor, Plot 3, Splendor Forum, Jasola District Centre, New Delhi – 110025, India

103 Penang Road, #05–06/07, Visioncrest Commercial, Singapore 238467

Cambridge University Press is part of Cambridge University Press & Assessment, a department of the University of Cambridge.

We share the University's mission to contribute to society through the pursuit of education, learning and research at the highest international levels of excellence.

www.cambridge.org
Information on this title: www.cambridge.org/9781009463010

DOI: 10.1017/9781009463027

First published 2024

A catalogue record for this publication is available from the British Library.

ISBN 978-1-009-46301-0 Paperback
ISSN 2514-8524 (online)
ISSN 2514-8516 (print)

Old Delhi's Parallel Book Bazaar

Elements in Publishing and Book Culture

DOI: 10.1017/9781009463027

First published online: November 2024

Kanupriya Dhingra

Author for correspondence: Kanupriya Dhingra, kanupriyadhingra.soas@gmail.com

ABSTRACT: This Element looks at Old Delhi's Daryaganj Sunday Book Market, popularly known as Daryaganj Sunday Patri Kitab Bazaar, as a parallel location for books and a site of resilience and possibilities. The first section studies the bazaar's spatiality: its location, relocation, and respatialisation. Three actors play a major role in creating and organising this spatiality: the sellers, the buyers, and the civic authorities. The second section narrativises the biographies of the booksellers of Daryaganj to offer a map of the hidden social and material networks that support the informal modes of bookselling. Amidst order and chaos, using their specialised knowledge, Daryaganj booksellers create distinctive mechanisms to serve the diverse reading public of Delhi. Using ethnography, oral interviews, and rhythmanalysis, this Element tells a story of urban aspirations, state–citizen relations, official and unofficial cultural economies, and imaginations of other viable worlds of being and believing.

This Element also has a video abstract: www.cambridge.org/dhingra_abstract

KEYWORDS: book bazaar, spatiality, street vendors, book history, ethnography

ISBNs: 9781009463010 (PB), 9781009463027 (OC)

ISSNs: 2514-8524 (online), 2514-8516 (print)

Contents

Introduction

This Element looks at Old Delhi's Daryaganj Sunday Book Market, popularly known as Daryaganj Sunday Patri Kitab Bazaar, as a parallel location for books and a site of resilience and possibilities. The first section studies the bazaar's spatiality: its location on the streets, its relocation to a gated compound called 'Mahila Haat', and its subsequent respatialisation. Three actors play a major role in creating and organising this spatiality: the sellers, the buyers, and the state. I study the bazaar in the precise moments of transformation when the pressures of municipal regulations and the neo-capitalist standardisation of urban space forced a semi-formal book bazaar into a bounded, formalised book market. The second section narrativises the biographies of book vendors to offer a map of the hidden social and material networks that support more informal modes of bookselling.

Located in Old Delhi (or Shahjanabad, as it was known when the city was founded), Daryaganj Sunday Book Market is a serendipitous site marked with a historical past that made it conducive to informal trade. I use ethnography, rhythmanalysis, and interviews conducted between June 2019 to February 2020 to argue that while selling books on the streets is not a new phenomenon, the uniqueness of this bazaar lies in its distinctive mechanisms and the specialisations of the booksellers of Daryaganj, and the significant role that these play in serving the speculative category of the reading public of Delhi. However, the very dynamics that have led to the commercial success of the Patri Kitab Bazaar – entrepreneurship opportunities for its booksellers, a healthy resale trade, and a growing urban population in need of affordable books – are also the dynamics that contribute to the increasing regulation of the city that threatens the continued existence of the bazaar.

Daryaganj Sunday Patri Kitab Bazaar runs on a combination of order and chaos. Despite the external and internal forms of regulation and boundary work, the bazaar depends on a serendipity derived from the space of the street. Its visually and culturally vibrant aesthetics comprise booksellers setting up their stalls (stall *sajana*, in Hindi) and pedestrians/book buyers walking around and buying books, which are arranged in neat stacks or placed together in heaps. The books that are 'found' on the streets of Daryaganj are a result of what I call 'double chance encounters', whereby the booksellers find books that make their way to their godowns (warehouses) and book stalls, and readers/pedestrians find these books at the book market. The search algorithms that this book market incorporates are marked by characteristics such as 'accident', 'arbitrariness', 'unpredictability', 'contingency', 'wonder', 'excitement', and 'randomness'. The *find* (n.) then embodies serendipity. However, as one of the booksellers exclaimed in an interview: 'There is a *machinery* working behind this market.'

This 'machinery' comprises three '*parallel*' communication circuits of *books* at the Patri Kitab Bazaar: (1) the 'traditional circuit', where used and rare books are sold; (2) the 'study-material circuit', which branched off from the traditional circuit, and which includes syllabus books and their ancillary, 'out-of-syllabus' books; and, finally, (3) the 'duplicate circuit', where pirated/duplicate books, or what the vendors call 'D *ki kitab*' are sold in various formats.[1] When books exit the 'proper' Darntonian circuit (1972) as waste, excess, or due to a shift in their utility, there is an alteration in the book's worth. Notably, in the case of South Asia, where informal and illicit markets often co-exist with formal and licit ones, the limitations of Darnton's model[2] can become the point of departure for the uncovering of the subsequent lives – or afterlives – of the book outside the Darntonian circuit.

In their afterlife, all books at the Daryaganj Sunday Book Bazaar are *nayi-jaisi*, or 'like new', and they are sold in a (recom)modified, parallel

---

[1] Kanupriya Dhingra, *Book History in India* series, volume four: this forthcoming book chapter is a detailed exploration of the three parallel circuits of Daryaganj Book Bazaar.

[2] Robert Darnton's seminal scholarly work provides us with three pivotal questions when confronted by the book object: 'How do books come into being? How do they reach readers? What do readers make of them?' With regard to the second question, Darnton believes that all printed books pass through the same 'life cycle' (What Is the History of Books? *Daedalus*, 111 (3), 65–83; 67). The principal actors in Darnton's circuit – which I refer to in this Element as the 'proper' communication circuit – are the author, the publisher and/or the bookseller, the printer, and other intermediaries such as suppliers, binders, and shippers. The site of a bookshop – or what I call the 'proper' bookshop – is the enabler of this circuit.

format: second-hand, rare, photocopied, or pirated. There are precise methods for evaluating a book's value when it leaves the proper circuit. A book's 'departure' is not fixed either. Daryaganj books, especially in the traditional circuit, exit from the proper model at various points. Books are sieved from an eclectic, hybrid stock of 'paper-waste' or *raddi*. They also arrive via the private libraries of readers from Delhi on their demise, or are discarded by public libraries and institutions. Then there is the cross-border trade in waste books: developing countries such as India are the wasteland for what the readers of the first world have conveniently discarded. Apart from ship equipment, garments, and e-waste, containers from the United States and the United Kingdom are also one of the earliest sources of books in Daryaganj. Remainder stock from publishers is another important source of books in Daryaganj. Once they are deemed inappropriate to enter the 'proper' market space, publishers auction books cheaply. The booksellers at Daryaganj also bought books from each other, creating value out of each other's sourced material.

Hence, the location of the book stalls on the pavements, the booksellers, the book buyers, their experience of selling and buying, and the marketing and circulation circuits of books in the bazaar are all *parallel* to the official, formal, more 'respectable' habitats of publishers, bookshops, chain stores, e-retail, and the like. 'Parallel', as opposed to 'proper', represents alternative trajectories, the elasticity of the circulation network, the characteristics of the books, the spatiality of the market, and the nature of the business.

Unlike in the West, where book history can productively draw on archival sources such as publishers' records, trade journals, catalogues, trade figures, and the like, South Asian book historians are constrained from the outset by a lack of such records. This is particularly true of post-independence India, where successive attempts to measure the size and scope of the book trade have yielded inadequate results. This is due not only to the lack of publishers' archives and the Indian practice of selling junk paper to the friendly neighbourhood *kabadiwallah* (paper merchant/scrap dealer), but also to the largely unregulated nature of the book market, which has grown in the current climate of desktop publishing and print-on-demand. To turn this lack into an advantage, drawing on my experience of the Sunday Book Bazaar, first as a buyer and then as a researcher, I have set my investigation within a primarily ethnographic framework.

Overall, I aim to preserve the stories of the bazaar and its booksellers to demonstrate how bookselling is shaped by and shapes local needs and contexts. This Element, then, calls for scholars to engage with the diverse modes and significant geographies of bookselling.

1 'Locating' the Sunday Book Bazaar

Vignette 1

On a Sunday morning, prior to 21 July 2019, you face the now-closed Golcha Cinema on Netaji Subhash Marg in Daryaganj, Old Delhi. You could be a local, a recent migrant to the city, or a tourist. On any other day, most of the regular shops on this road are open, selling medical equipment or musical instruments, located alongside publishers' offices, sex clinics, local and multinational food joints, and a government-owned beer and wine shop. On Sundays, most of the regular shops and offices on this busy commercial road are shut for their weekly day off. Instead, starting from around 9 a.m., you spot a flea market on the footpath (or *patri*) that spills over to cover the closed shutters of the shops behind them. Like any other weekly bazaar in Delhi, there is an elongated line of vendors on the sidewalk. That line has a dominant and rather distinct visual presence. It has changed how Daryaganj looks on any other day of the week. It is because of this line of vendors – most of whom are selling only books – that the *patri* is occupied by pedestrians, in much higher numbers than on weekdays. Most are here to buy books. The books they are after are laid out on the ground or have been creatively arranged by vendors – either neatly on the ground so that the titles are visible to the walkers or heaped together with distinct, colourful signs declaring their price per kilo or per book. The books are of various kinds and varying degrees of newness. Their diversity matches the diverse ways in which the books are displayed and priced at each bookstall. The bookstalls attract casual pedestrians and the regular Daryaganj afficionados (or *shauqeens*) whose motion may be arrested by a title they see. They bend over one stall after another. You walk towards the crowd to become part of it.

Further on, as you walk along Netaji Subhash Marg, you also encounter a few bookshops, both makeshift and permanent, along the sidewalk. These are quite unlike the regular bookshops you might see across Delhi, such as the famous Bahrisons at its original location in Khan Market or its new branches in Select City Walk Mall in Saket or Ambience Mall in Vasant Kunj, or The Bookshop in Lodhi Colony – all shiny mirrors and air-conditioned coolness.

The bookshops on Netaji Subhash Marg have a milieu similar to the stalls on the *patri*: books are piled together, mostly divided by genre, on elevated surfaces covered with paper or cloth. The prices are fixed, and books are sold by weight, unless they are 'rare books'. To learn the price of these rare books, you must ask the bookshop owner. Some of the crowd on the *patri* enter these bookshops as well. One could claim that the bookstalls look like an extension of these bookshops, only we know which came first: the stalls. You might have spotted similar stalls or bookshops on the smaller lanes leading into Daryaganj via Netaji Subhash Marg. As you follow the trail of book vendors on the footpath leading towards Delhi Gate (or *Dilli Gate/Dilli Darwaza*), you turn right onto the sidewalks of Asaf Ali Marg. You continue walking from Delhi Gate Metro Station, exit number 3, and do not stop until you have reached Delite Cinema, which, like Golcha, is one of the city's historic cinema halls. Here, the line of booksellers ends.

If, as you walk from Golcha Cinema to Delite, you find a book that interests you – because it is old and/or inexpensive, your grandmother had a copy, or for any other peculiar or personal reason – you buy it. You might also have to bargain here unless you buy it from the 'fixed price' lot. You could have exited the book market at any point since it has no specific beginning or end, despite the fixed geographical span. This L-shaped market was known as Daryaganj Sunday Patri Kitab Bazaar until it was shut down in July 2019, and relocated, in September 2019, renamed as 'Sunday Book Bazaar, Mahila Haat'.

Vignette 2

On a Sunday morning, soon after 28 September 2019, you walk out of one of the exit gates of Delhi Gate Metro Station and into Daryaganj. You look for the book market on the pavements. Instead, you find very few booksellers with hardly any books lying before them, who tell you that this is all that is left of the Daryaganj Sunday Patri Kitab Bazaar. What are they still doing here, you ask. They tell you, or you overhear some of them telling the media, that they are raising their voice against the Municipal Corporation of Delhi (MCD) to retain the footpaths of Netaji Subhash Marg and Asaf Ali Marg as the official vending zone for second-hand books. They have been struggling for the last two months and now the bazaar has been relocated. It is evident that most booksellers are dissatisfied with the relocation. '*Beti Bachao Beti Parhao: Bina Kitab Ke Kaise Parhegi Beti?*' ('Save the girl child, educate the girl child: How will she study without books?') is one of several slogans they have put on display (Figure 11). The book vendors claim that Daryaganj Sunday Patri Kitab Bazaar was an institution and part of the larger education economy in the city and the country. You are given a pamphlet explaining their struggle. Nostalgia for the street is still brewing inside the bookshops that used to be extensions of the *patri* (footpath) bookstalls: the bookshops at Netaji Subhash Marg are unusually crowded, with buyers lining up to the cash counter. Most of the buyers used to purchase their weekly stock of books from the Patri Kitab Bazaar and are now flocking to the bookshops that, in the absence of the Sunday Book Bazaar, carry on the same book trading tradition.

Suppose you are more informed since you have followed the news about the relocation via online or print reports. In that case, you walk further along Asaf Ali Marg to the Broadway Hotel, another significant landmark in the Old City. This is where you spot 'Mahila Haat': the new, officially designated location for the sale of second-hand books in Delhi and an alternative to the Daryaganj Sunday Patri Kitab Bazaar.[3] You enter the Haat from the only entry gate, which leads to an elevated platform. (There is a second gate at the other end of the Haat, but it is not in use.) Along the stairs, a newly built pavement allows rickshaws and lorries to enter the book market so that books from the nearby storage units that belong to the booksellers can be brought in, although with much difficulty and labour. Once you've climbed the stairs, you can see a book market, all at once. The stalls are spread across the length and bredth of the bazaar. There are numbers painted on the marble floor, and the whole platform is marked and divided into uniform rectangles, six feet wide by four feet long, outlined with yellow paint. The books here are arranged in similar yet somewhat diverse ways compared to the streets. Some booksellers are exploring novel practices, such as putting books on low, elongated tables

---

[3] In Hindi, 'haat' refers to a quasi-permanent marketplace.

instead of directly on the ground or building forts with the spines of the books facing outwards or inwards and the bookseller standing inside to guide you through them and negotiate the price. Some stalls have installed tall umbrellas to protect the bookseller from the sunlight, as well as other accessories such as standing bookshelves and stools, which were not previously used in the Patri Kitab Bazaar. As you walk inside the Haat, you find a book that interests you – because it is old and inexpensive, your grandmother had a copy, or for any other peculiar or personal reason – and you buy it. It is possible that you had to bargain here as well unless you bought it from the 'fixed price' lot. You exit from the same gate you had entered as and when it pleases you, without necessarily having explored the furthest corners of Mahila Haat.

These two vignettes offer a glimpse of what the Sunday Patri Kitab Bazaar looked like on the streets of Daryaganj and how the experience is being recreated inside Mahila Haat by the sellers, the buyers, and the civic authorities – the three actors of the bazaar – even if only partially. Building on these visual samples of the appearance, experience, and rhythms of the two incarnations of the book bazaar, this section focuses on their spatiality: what goes into making the character of the space of the book bazaar, before and after its relocation, and the experience of being inside and traversing these spaces, or what I call 'locating' these book markets. The act and process of 'locating' is a three-way engagement between several actors: booksellers, book buyers, and civic authorities.

Over time, booksellers have periodically turned some streets in Daryaganj into a book market by negotiating with the available urban space. The civic authorities have regulated (and continue to regulate) the use of this space, forcing, pushing, or prompting the sellers to create new, additional patterns of occupation. The book buyers who have motivated the creation of these official and unofficial patterns of occupation and navigated through them are, I feel, rather unacknowledged participants in the geographical and sensory dimensions that the space of the street has to offer. I will discuss how these actors have enabled the spatialisation of the streets of Daryaganj into a *parallel* book bazaar such that the book bazaar created distinguishable rhythms of its own, simultaneously merging with and divorced from the regular rhythms of the total space of Daryaganj.

1.1 Streets and Serendipity: A 'Natural' Book Bazaar

There are several origin stories for the book bazaar. The now-relocated market is said to have operated since the Mughal Empire. Akbarabadi Mahal, emperor Shahjahan's wife, built Faiz Bazaar near Dilli Darwaza (Delhi Gate) in its earliest form in CE 1650: 'a 1050-gaz-long and 30-gaz-wide bazaar', confirms Sayyid Ahmed Khan in *Asār-Us-Sanadid*. 'It had stone shops on both sides, and a canal used to flow in the centre.'[4] The name *Daryaganj* means 'a market across a river', where *Darya* refers to a river (here, the river Yamuna) and *Ganj* refers to a site where trade is conducted. It was not always the same product that was traded here. Daryaganj only became synonymous with the sale of used, rare, pirated books in the 1960s. According to locals, Daryaganj started as a consumer goods market adjacent to the walls between Subhash Park and Kasturba Gandhi Hospital. There were vinyl records and record players, radios, transistors, mechanical goods, medical goods, and used clothes; books, too, found their place. After a few minor relocations not significantly far away from the lanes of Daryaganj, a few booksellers moved to the now absent *Lohe ka Pul* (Iron Bridge), near Golcha Cinema, from where the street market began to expand. Before its recent relocation to a nearby site named Mahila Haat, the bazaar extended to Delite Cinema Hall. The market structure was shaped like a long 'L', with books stacked on the sidewalks of Netaji Subhash Marg and Asaf Ali Marg, and it hosted more than 250 vendors (Figure 1).

The identity of the place surrounding Daryaganj, especially near Delhi Gate and behind Red Fort, has been associated with various marketplaces or 'bazaars', such as Sadar Bazaar, Urdu Bazaar, Chawri Bazaar, Chandni Chowk, and Nai Sarak, to name a few. While this historical past has made the streets attractive to small-scale entrepreneurs and prospective vendors, serendipity has played a role in the making and operation of the Sunday Book Bazaar for the last six decades. In fact, as the book bazaar became more established, the commercial locality became associated with second-hand books, and not only on Sundays. In other words, there developed a collective understanding among the city dwellers (the *Dilliwallah*) and even

[4] C. M. Naim. 'Syed Ahmad and his two books called 'Asar-al-Sanadid'.' *Modern Asian Studies* 45.3 (2011): 669–708.

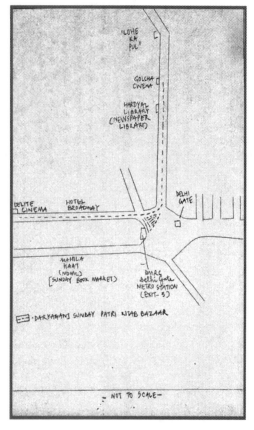

Figure 1 A sketch of the L-Shaped Sunday Book Market on the streets of Daryaganj.

national and international travellers to associate the Daryaganj streets with being a place for books.[5] The function of these streets also began to change

[5] Not so far from the Sunday Book Bazaar in Daryaganj, Ansari Road stands out as the definitive hub for publishers in Delhi since independence, and Nai Sarak

accordingly. Shops for second-hand books, such as the Mukta Book Agency, opened in the vicinity. Some footpath booksellers turned their parallel book business into a relatively 'proper' model of selling books: Delhi Book Store on Ansari Road, Jacksons in Paharganj, and Om Books International (now a major commercial publisher) are a few examples.

Serendipity has also played a significant role in many a patri book vendor's professional trajectory. Your regular Daryaganj book vendor might have been a freelance photographer, an Urdu lecturer, a New Delhi Municipal Council (NDMC) official, a rickshaw puller, a newspaper hawker, a vegetable seller, an embroiderer, a copyeditor, a stenographer, and so on. Most of them found their way to books 'by chance', they told me, with a sense of surprise at how they have survived in the business as to start with, and for a long time, they did not assume that this would be their long-term profession. Many booksellers have been in the business for decades. They have engaged with the available space to take advantage of the opportunity that the streets offer to benefit their business. In the case of book buyers, beyond their serendipitous 'finds' of the day, walking becomes a creative gesture that helps them spatialise the Patri Kitab Bazaar. Meanwhile, the civic authorities have strived to regulate these creative arrangements, with Mahila Haat as the most recent and, so far, the most organised result of such regulation.

1.1.1 Organising Serendipity: The Booksellers of Daryaganj

Since Daryaganj Sunday Patri Kitab Bazaar used to be set up on the footpath (or *patri*), the sale of books in this location can be officially understood as 'street vending'. Street vending engages with intentional as well as incidental buyers. In this case, the incidental buyer is someone who may or may not have intended to come to that market or to buy the books sold at the Patri

serves as a book market for textbooks. These two locations epitomise formalised book distribution in Old Delhi. Urdu Bazaar near Jama Masjid is the main publishing, printing, and selling market for new, old, and rare books and magazines in Urdu and Farsi. See Rashmi Sadana, *English Heart, Hindi Heartland: The Political Life of Literature in India* (Permanent Black, 2012), and Rimi B. Chatterjee, *Empires of the Mind: A History of the Oxford University Press in India Under the Raj* (Oxford University Press, 2006).

Kitab Bazaar. For both the incidental and the regular buyers, the vendors adopt strategies such that when these buyers walk past and see the goods in the bazaar, they feel a desire for a specific article. This forms an integral part of their body of knowledge and specialisation as second-hand booksellers (*kitab-vikreta*) at Daryaganj. This moment of visual contact is provoked by a series of random and planned events, and we may call the whole sequence of seeing, stopping, and/or buying 'serendipitous'.

Figures 2 and 3 represent typical bookstalls at the Patri Kitab Bazaar – their characteristic aesthetic sense and minimal infrastructure. As a part of their knowledge and specialisation, booksellers are aware that *stall sajana*, or curating book displays at their stalls, can help capture the fleeting attention of the passer-by, and that it is through such visual engagement that the sale of books occurs in the first place. That is, a potential buyer must first see the book to establish the desire to buy it since, unless their bookstall is only selling one kind of book, the vendor can establish only a minimally

Figure 2 Bookstalls on Netaji Subhash Marg, near Delhi-Gate (September 2017).

Figure 3 *Stall Sajana* (Setting up a stall) – Netaji Subhash Marg (September 2017).

coherent arrangement by genre, type, or 'age' of the books. Booksellers go for optimum utilisation of the pitch that they regularly occupy and try to attract buyers through their display, either by piling the books together for an attractive price (mostly by weight) or by neatly displaying each cover so that a passer-by stops or a potential buyer's gaze browses while looking for their find of the day as they walk by (Figures 2, 3, 4, 5).

The booksellers adopt different methods of arranging books on their stalls. Displaying the covers of the books is one way to capture the attention of buyers. These are the books whose price is negotiable. In most cases, books stacked in heaps carry the same price. Figure 7 shows how the vendors use signs and placards. Books could be for '*Ek Dam*' ('each book is for the same price') or all for the same price ('Sale, 50/-' – Each book on sale for Rs. 50). Sellers often go creative, with exclamations such as '*Fix Price Matlab No Tension*' ('fixed price means no tension'). There are other requests and alerts: '*Kripya Mol Bhav Na Karein*' ('kindly avoid negotiation'), or 'take care of your belongings'. The booksellers kept revising their strategies as the use and the outlook of the streets are modified by the state with new construction or new policies, time and again. For instance, the bookstalls shown in Figure 4 are located right outside the Delhi Gate Metro Station, exit number 3. The booksellers began to occupy the area around the exit gate as soon as the metro station was built. Even while construction was underway, the booksellers continued to set up their stalls around the barricades.

A regular buyer may be able to identify these patterns of the stalls and their wares and approach the bazaar bookstalls accordingly. With repeated

Figure 4 Bookstalls outside Delhi Gate Metro Station, Exit number 3 (July 2019).

Figure 5 Arrangement of the bookstalls on Asaf Ali Marg using the closed shutters of the offices that run on weekdays (July 2019).

visits, they would know what to expect from the stalls where the covers are displayed individually, as against the heaps of books, which mostly meant that they had to search through them. This is quite unlike the planned and organised arrangement and categorisation within a 'proper' bookshop, where books are sold as per the market price. Unlike the repeat buyers who have over a period noted the bookstalls where they are more likely to find a desirable book, it is primarily the new or incidental buyer who must be lured 'towards' the bookstall – and not 'inside', as is the case with a proper bookshop.

Unlike the presence of a threshold in a 'proper' bookstore, the territory of a stall is outlined by the books laid out on the streets. There are also other makeshift paraphernalia: minimal structural stability and maximum provisionality characterise the space of a bookstall, as opposed to the bookstore space. For instance, Dilshad Ali brings iron boxes full of used English novels, the national favourite *Raj Comics* and the international favourite *Asterix*, and books by popular Hindi authors such as Surendra Mohan Pathak. He uses the same boxes as book-display platforms. In Figure 6, we see a bookseller arranging his stock in cardboard boxes outside the Hindi Book Centre (Star Publishing Group), which is closed on Sundays. He uses the same cardboard boxes as a surface on which to display the books. At the end of the day, he packs the books away in the same boxes. As the serendipitous visual contact occurs, this determines whether the buyer desires to buy a book, quickly gauging its 'sacral value' before entering

Figure 6 *Stall Sajana* – Asaf Ali Marg (July 2019).

Figure 7 Pricing the books (Juy 2017).

into the bargaining process. (Ali marks the prices of used books with a pencil, thus retaining the possibility of negotiation.) Hence, I argue that this bazaar's literary experience relies significantly on the serendipity resulting from how the bookseller utilises the space of the street and how buyers navigate their passage across it.

1.1.2 Mapping the Bazaar: The Walkers of Daryaganj

Walking is key to the experience of book buying at the Patri Kitab Bazaar. On Sundays, as they browse, pause, purchase, or ignore some bookstalls, book buyers become part of an indeterminate city crowd, withdrawing from it from time to time. As the bookstalls make the bazaar 'visible', the book buyers spatialise it by their movement and engagement. As seen in Vignette 1, the footpath is an open space that allows for an accessible conglomeration of multiple rhythms. Several rhythms run parallel, and others (like those of

the Patri Kitab Bazaar) thrive on the absence of a few. The possibility for
a pedestrian to simultaneously participate in and avoid any of these rhythms
creates a serendipitous space for book purchase and sale. Here, the walker
gains agency in creating their own ways of negotiating with serendipity and
order. While the street is brimming with pedestrians on weekdays and
weekends alike, I will highlight how walking on the footpath specifically on
Sundays gains a catalytic and 'creative' meaning.

In my interviews, several Daryaganj *shauqeens* and other regular buyers
spoke of how the book bazaar offered them a 'unique experience' compared
to bookshops. This uniqueness is courtesy of the accidental nature of
finding the market on the streets and their 'find of the day', and how such
serendipitous encounters often lead to their *lagaav* (attachment) to the space
and its books over repeated visits. Except for students, Daryaganj regulars
rarely came to the Daryaganj Patri Kitab Bazaar hoping to find a specific
book. Students, too, were offered an abundance of variety in terms of
a book's editions – low-end or high-end textbooks, along with several
additional out-of-syllabus books – all of which are very helpful in meeting
the demands of the schools and colleges of Delhi, as well as the coaching
institutes for various competitive exams mushrooming throughout the
capital city.[6] Moreover, buyers could not predict the quantity or the type
of books on offer. The chaos stirred the hope that you might find something
you were looking for or something you never thought you wanted in the
first place. That joy!

However, upon studying the rhythms of the Patri Kitab Bazaar – by
recording the market events on camera or in the traditional manner of
keeping notes in my diary and analysing them retrospectively – I observed
that there may be specific patterns that the walkers have developed. Despite
the seemingly fixed 'L-shape' that the market had acquired, starting from
Golcha Cinema on Netaji Subhash Marg to Delite Cinema on Asaf Ali

[6] Sadana writes about the cropping up of coaching centres in Delhi, which constitutes one of the diverse forms of 'aspirational planning that ultimately privilege
and enact a notion of upward mobility rather than social equality'. See Rashmi
Sadana, "We Are Visioning It': Aspirational Planning and the Material
Landscapes of Delhi's Metro'. *City & Society* (2018) 186–209.

Marg, regular buyers did not necessarily follow this trail in a linear fashion. They chose their entry and exit points depending on where the stalls they liked were positioned. Repeat buyers had created their own trails. Among those, it was likely for, say, students from various universities in Delhi to bring their friends along and make them follow the same trails. (Some buyers would also know which local, nearby *dhaba* they would eat at before or after spending their day at the Patri Kitab Bazaar.) Nevertheless, any amount of planning still retains the possibility of the surprises that each stall may offer.

While inside the bazaar, I noticed how new buyers usually attempted to make sense of the whole landscape, trying to understand and take in the apparent disorder. A new visitor found that starting from the first stall at either end of the book market was relatively 'safe'. The buyer from Vignette 1, who joins the crowd from Golcha Cinema, is a typical example. It is easier to follow the trail of the bazaar, in that sense, and not get overwhelmed. Non-buyers, including anyone who is not buying books from the stalls, were often seen wanting to escape the trail of booksellers altogether, choosing not to walk on the footpaths and walking on the edge of the road instead. Therefore, there are indeed ways in which a buyer may *spatialise* the Patri Kitab Bazaar, and these ways are manifold when compared to the limited scope of creativity of movement in a bookshop.

With every time-lapse recording of the bazaar, my faith in the book buyers grew stronger: they indeed spatialise the bazaar by simply walking on the streets – their movements and pauses and where they choose to be on the footpaths, amidst a mixed crowd. The grids on a map of this area will show a continuous and coherent way a pedestrian can walk these streets. However, in this periodically recurring space, buyers and non-buyers create their own patterns and individual strategies. As much as the booksellers try to define the Patri Kitab Bazaar by adapting to the space of the street as they do with their strategic movements, the buyer's role is equally significant in this process of spatialisation. There is no one way to enter or exit the bazaar, and it seems that the walker can choose to be present or absent from the market while in that area. They could move in and out of it while perpetually being *in the proximity* of the book market, whether they decide to participate or not. There is an absence of a threshold to the bookstalls, even though the sellers try to set a boundary for their stall. (Some buyers hop on to the booksellers' side, crossing the implied boundary that the bookseller has established.) But it is the buyer's engagement – their movements, pauses, interactions, and even ignorance – that, in a way, *frames* a Daryaganj bookstall.

A buyer's movements and activities were a spatial enactment of the book market and the geographical area of Daryaganj/the area around Delhi Gate. In other words, much like the booksellers who created a parallel pattern to experience the space of the book markets and, by extension, the space of Daryaganj, the walkers enabled those patterns through their movement and engagement. Hence, walking was a performative gesture that enabled the parallel communication circuits at the bazaar. Unlike in a bookshop, in the absence of a threshold, it is the movement on the streets, the back-and-forth motion of the pedestrians simultaneously inside and/or outside the Patri Kitab Bazaar, that actualises the presence of the book bazaar. Hence, much like the sellers, the buyers contribute to creating a map of the Patri Kitab Bazaar.

Michel de Certeau has studied the act of walking in the city as a 'creative form of resistance'.[7] De Certeau's walker – or *Wandersmänner*, as he calls them – is an 'ordinary practitioner of the city' whose body follows 'the thicks and thins of an urban "text" they write without being able to read it'.[8] He argues that the progression of a walker on the streets is tactical since it is never entirely determined by the plans of organising bodies. A regular book buyer in Daryaganj, then, essentially resists the predetermined grids of a city. I noticed one especially intriguing way in which the spatiality of Patri Kitab Bazaar offered an experience beyond that of book buying. Patri Kitab Bazaar is an '*adda*'[9] in the city. Students mingled with friends or enjoyed

---

[7] Michel de Certeau, *The Practice of Everyday Life* (Berkeley: University of California Press, 1984).

[8] Ibid.

[9] Defined as a cultural spot for gathering, mingling, and conversations. See chapter 1 in Bhaswati Bhattarchrya, 'Adda and Public Spaces of Sociability before the ICH', in *MuchAado Over Coffee : Indian Coffee House Then and Now* (Routledge, 2018).

solitary walks in the bazaar and the Old City. Srivastava, in *Passionate Modernity*, points to the likelihood of strangers meeting in an urban land-scape beyond the gaze of intimates.[10] Anonymity in the crowd is a risk for parents with younger children, who they fear will get lost as they go from one stall to another. Even if their children had little role to play in the decision-making and negotiation, I often saw parents holding hands or asking their children to stay in sight. Some parents encourage their children to browse the books while discouraging them from buying the expensive ones – that is not why one comes to the Sunday Book Bazaar. Conversely, older (unsupervised) students were on their own as they roamed from one stall to another. This is probably why they are more likely to go beyond the stalls providing study material and bump into a book they didn't intend to buy – a second-hand novel or a fashion magazine. The anonymity also helped young lovers to hold hands – not to prevent their partners from wandering off, but to keep them close in a city where public displays of affection aren't an easy pursuit. In this way, Patri Kitab Bazaar's openness, despite the crowds and the chaos, offered intimacy through anonymity.

While walking is indeed a key form of experiencing the Patri Kitab Bazaar, it is also a significant part of a seller's specialised knowledge: for instance, deciding what part of the street will receive most footfall or how to create visual incentives for the pedestrians. However, the possibility of having agency is limited since civic authorities – the third actors, who officially decide the spatialisation of the streets of Daryaganj – play a decisive role. This will become clear when I discuss the events of 2019, when the Patri Kitab Bazaar was relocated. Despite their efforts to retain the bazaar on the streets, the sellers and buyers could not stop the authorities from removing it. Further, even in determining the new location of the bazaar at Mahila Haat, the sellers and buyers had minimal say in the final decision. Time and again, the civic authorities have demonstrated their control over the Kitab Bazaar, by controlling the book buyers' presence and movement, as well as limiting their agency to spatialise or 'locate' the bazaar.

---

[10] Sanjay Srivastava, *Passionate Modernity: Sexuality, Class, and Consumption in India* (Routledge, 2007), p. 290.

1.1.3 Regulating Serendipity: The Civic Authorities

Serendipity coexists with regulation and organisation at the bazaar. The vendors create order amidst the chaos of the street to create a space for the Patri Kitab Bazaar, to make it locatable. The stalls are arranged one after the other to create a trail, and each stall is set up using minimal materials – whether this is the use of cardboard boxes for marking the boundary of a stall or an inverted umbrella to provide shade to the bookseller and inadvertently highlight the presence of the stall (Figures 6 and 3, respectively). Walkers organise the bazaar via their creative tactics, formed after repeated visits. However, the official regulation of this serendipity that comes under the purview of the civic authorities has always created tensions.[11] It is this dynamic between order and chaos on the streets of Daryaganj that I will discuss here.

Daryaganj Sunday Patri Kitab Bazaar has been distinguished from the other local weekly markets that are set up periodically 'by the poor for the poor' across various locations in Delhi; these are also referred to in the Street Vendor's Act 2014 as LWMs.[12] In the Act, the book bazaar is recorded as a *specialised* weekly market, as distinct from any other local weekly market, since it hosts the sale of one specific good (i.e. books) across the breadth of the street market. At other local weekly markets across the city, vendors sell a diverse variety of goods, such as clothes, footwear, kitchen utensils, sports equipment, everyday cleaning essentials, and so forth. Further, Daryaganj

---

[11] While the complete removal of the market space is a clear threat to the street vendors' livelihoods, informal markets have been dealing with rather subtle fears as a part of their everyday business routine. For instance, it is usual for the vendors at New Delhi's Sarojini Nagar market – the largest market for affordable clothes and fashion accessories in India – to 'clean up' the sections of their stalls that encroach on public space, knowing that the police could arrive at specific hours of the day. As long as the encroachment is not *seen* by the authorities, the shopkeepers are excused from the fine that they would otherwise have to pay for setting up their shops outside the officially designated area. The vendors at Daryaganj book market always found themselves on the safer side as far as the everyday evacuation was concerned.

[12] See the copy of the Act here: www.mohua.gov.in/upload/uploadfiles/files/StreetVendorAct2014_English(1).pdf.

Sunday Patri Kitab Bazaar has been officially registered as a 'natural market' by the North Delhi Municipal Corporation of Delhi (NrDMC). the administrative body that controls the regulated and non-regulated spaces in North Delhi. In the Street Vendors (Protection of Livelihood and Regulation of Street Vending) Act, 2014, a natural market is defined as 'a market where sellers and buyers have traditionally congregated for the sale and purchase of products or services and has been determined as such by the local authority on the recommendations of the Town Vending Committee'. In other words, it is a space established over time where buyers and sellers interact without significant institutional intervention. So, it's safe to say – and is perhaps even officially sanctioned – that the book bazaar exemplified serendipity. In other words, the official Act recognises the *bazaaris'*[13] autonomy and the bazaar's serendipity.

There has been a desire amongst the vendors to legitimise their trade on the streets, and for that, they undertook certain actions. Throughout the course of its several relocations, Daryaganj Sunday Patri Kitab Bazaar has managed to negotiate with institutional regulation, planning, and supervision in wonderful and creative ways: from how the books were procured to the moderately regulated positioning of the bookstalls and the erratic and inventive movement of the buyers. All this made the market into what it is and shaped its rhythms, in which randomness happens *despite* what the booksellers here identify as censorship. In fact, the vendors associate regulation with '*pabandi*' (restraint) and '*shoshan*' (exploitation, censorship), valuing the role of serendipity in the establishment and operation of their business.[14]

---

[13] Translation: the people of the bazaar.

[14] As Suvrata Chowdhary explains, 'the term "authorised" suggests that the street where the weekly market is organised gets the no objection certification from the MCD, henceforth MCD collects rent for the use of the space from the vendors. It also gives notional protection from police harassment. A market which is unauthorised is vulnerable to police extortion for money from the vendors and if vendors are not able to pay then their goods are confiscated, or they are beaten up. Hence weekly market organisers in unauthorised spaces try to get their markets formalised.' See Suvrata Chowdhary (2017), 'The Local Weekly

In Delhi, 97 per cent of the state's population comes under the jurisdiction of the Municipal Corporation of Delhi (MCD). The MCD is responsible for implementing national policy and for regularising street vending in the national capital. Before 2011, the street vendors received a pink receipt, or *gulabi parchi,* from the MCD. This *parchi* noted the fee they paid to the civic authorities to occupy the streets. In 2011, the sale of books on the streets of Daryaganj was legalised through the *tehbazaari* system, with the help of the Self-Employed Women's Association (SEWA).[15] *Tehbazaari* is a licence for the grantee to squat at a notified site on a pavement to conduct business. Since then, the market has been run by an elected body called 'Darya Ganj Patri Sunday Book Bazaar Welfare Association'.[16] This Association was formed as a representative body for the vendors. A president, vice-president, registrar, and cashier were elected by the vendors from among themselves, whereby redressals related to the vendors' stalls, their location, the stock, or weighty issues such as relocation and shutting down could be addressed officially. With the increase in population and growing traffic concerns, most bazaars were gradually marked as 'encroachments' in an aspiring 'world' city. The events that led to the relocation of Daryaganj Sunday Patri Kitab Bazaar to its new location inside Mahila Haat exemplify the conflict of interest between the sellers

Markets of Delhi: Operating in the Formal "Space" and Informal Economy', *E-journal of the Indian Sociological Society,* 3–31, pp. 28.

[15] Since 2005, SEWA has aided vendors in establishing a welfare association with the Delhi government, guiding the market committee, ensuring their legitimacy, and securing legal rights that protected them from eviction threats. In 2011, when the police disallowed the market's operation, citing reasons such as traffic congestion and theft, SEWA collaborated with the DC and the Assistant Commissioner of Police (ACP), persuading them of the market's significant value. Subsequently, the market was allowed to resume its activities. In 2015, SEWA Delhi again played a pivotal role in assisting vendors with renewing their registration.

[16] With the relocation, this elected body was dismantled, and the previous president of the association has been arbitrarily assigned several responsibilities, such as location of space within the book market and that of legal arrangements between the booksellers and the civic authorities.

and the civic authorities. What happened on the streets of Daryaganj between July and September 2019?

Less than four weeks after starting my fieldwork in Daryaganj Sunday Patri Kitab Bazaar, it was lifted off the streets. Based on a Delhi High Court order dated 3 July 2019, the NrDMC mandated that the street market be removed, citing 'traffic concerns'.[17] Netaji Subhash Marg, which housed a part of Daryaganj Sunday Book Bazaar, was declared a non-vending zone. In a display of solidarity, vendors on Asaf Ali Marg (which did not come under the purview of the High Court order) also decided not to set up their stalls since all vendors could not have been accommodated on this street alone (only a part of the previous L-shape). For two months after the displacement, the vendors were left waiting for a decision on whether their stalls would be reinstated or whether they would be offered an alternative space.[18] Each passing week caused them a further loss of livelihood and made them increasingly desperate. To bypass the *pabandi*, several booksellers were seen adopting inventive ways of selling books from inconspicuous spaces to avoid confiscation – even inside an autorickshaw (Figure 9). One of the booksellers was also helped by the residents in the area. They allowed him to display his books inside their house, so the vendor asked one of his helpers to stand on the main street of Netaji Subhash Marg to bring in customers. The booksellers held several public protests (Figure 11). In one of the protests the vendors formed a human chain on Asaf Ali Marg. In another, they collected hundreds of testimonies from visitors dismayed at discovering that the market was absent from the streets yet again.

Even on past occassions of threats of relocation of the book bazaar, the vendors had claimed the 'natural' status of the book bazaar on these streets (as per the Street Vendors Act), and did not shy away from any official examination of its natural status. This was one of their principal demands

---

[17] Kanupriya Dhingra, 'Will Delhi Soon Have a Daryaganj-Used-Books-Market-Shaped Hole?', *Scroll.in*; 'Delhi's Daryaganj Book Bazaar Has a New, Sanitised Home, Which Has Benefits as Well as Drawbacks', *Scroll.in*; 'The Death of a Book Bazaar', *Himal Southasian*.

[18] Several newspaper reports covered the plight of the vendors caused by the delay in the process of redressal.

during the 2019 protests. The book vendors were striving to have the book bazaar's historical importance recognised, which would legitimise its existence on the streets, as against the closed, controlled space of Mahila Haat. The vendors stated that the market eviction had effectively violated the Street Vendors' Act and the recently formulated Street Vendors' Scheme, 2019. They claimed that the eviction of vendors without the recently formed Town Vending Committees first conducting a survey to map the selling conducted in that area (as mandated by the Street Vendor's Act) was a violation of the principal premise of the legislation and the older Street Vendor's Act. Several elements were significant in the events relating to the relocation in September 2019. For one, this was the first instance in more than fifty years that the Patri Kitab Bazaar had been forced to relocate. The market has been shut down in the past, notably in 1991, in 2005, and again for a few weeks in 2018 around Republic Day, mostly on the basis of similar concerns: traffic and illegal encroachment of streets. However, in July 2019, there was a larger concern looming for the vendors. The civic authorities had recently begun implementing instructions and procedures for the 'beautification' and sanitisation of the capital city.[19] The resilience shown by the booksellers to stay on the streets of Old Delhi highlighted the significance of their presence there, since that is where the birth and the evolution of bookselling in Daryaganj had occurred in the first place. When the civic authorities failed to recall the same, the vendors categorised this official and unilateral exercising of authority as '*shoshan*' or censorship.

As weeks passed, the vendors realised that the risk was more critical: that this time, the market might shut down for good or get relocated to a rather inconvenient and unprofitable location. As a result, they intensified their protests. They sought better attention from the press, as well as social media, where hashtags such as 'save book bazaar Daryaganj' and 'reclaim Sunday book bazaar' became popular. The booksellers were joined by community artists, academics, architects, students, and long-term regular visitors of Daryaganj Sunday Patri Kitab Bazaar, along with

---

[19] Proposal by Shahjahanabad Redevelopment Corporation, GNCT of Delhi: https://srdc.delhi.gov.in/sites/default/files/generic_multiple_files/revitaliza tion_of_shahjahanabad_project_concept_proposal.pdf.

some locals from the area and the city – also highlighting the bazaar's symbolic importance for the city dwellers (Figure 10). So, of the three actors – the sellers, the buyers, and the civic authorities – the two active participants were unwilling to let go of the streets. The protests lasted in this manner for two months, until the relocation. At this point, the vendors divided themselves into two groups.

The first group included those who migrated to Mahila Haat. These booksellers saw Mahila Haat as an upgrade of sorts. For them, it was a futuristic approach, whereby the new space promised betterment and improvement from their previous manner and methods of work. The new gated location was, apparently, to be well looked after, away from the nuisance that any street in Old Delhi may sustain. 'There will be no pickpocketing here, and women should move freely too', said Qamar Saeed, President of the Daryaganj Sunday Book Bazaar Welfare Association (Figure 8).[20] It would be a regulated space. Based on the national street vending policies, the booksellers were provided with a fixed area of 6×4 feet on a rental basis. The rent would be fixed at approximately Rs. 175 to Rs. 200 per week, which was increased by 10 per cent when the agreement was renewed after three years in 2023. The second group comprised vendors who decided to stay on the streets and fight for their space on the pavements. They saw the relocation as a loss of 'a thing of the past'. These vendors attached certain credibility to the history of the space, conducive to informal trade. They were suspicious of what the new site would offer and highly critical of the procedures that were followed for the relocation.

With only a few books lying on the ground and selling at the lowest price possible, these vendors were seen to be consciously diverting the readers and book buyers from the new location at Mahila Haat. The vendors claimed that officials from the MCD frequently confiscated their books, mostly without even providing them with the mandatory paperwork. The protesting booksellers became used to the Sisyphean task of laying down the books on the streets of Asaf Ali Marg and Netaji Subhash Marg, rushing away upon the arrival of MCD officials, laying down the books again, and

[20] See https://sundaybookbazar.com.

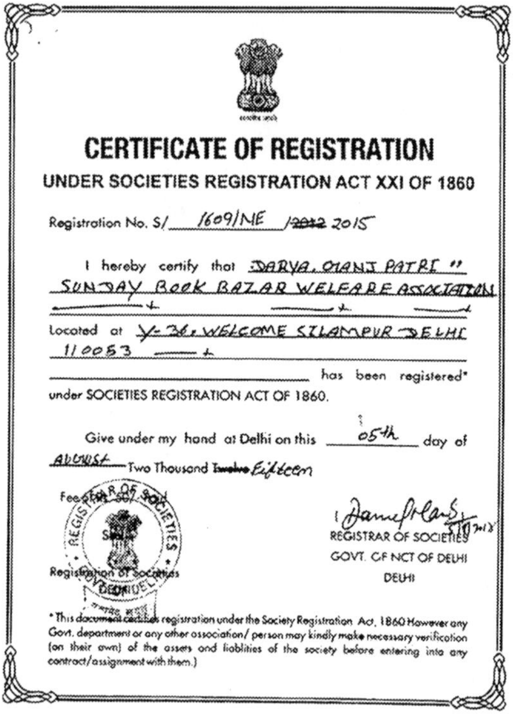

CERTIFICATE OF REGISTRATION

UNDER SOCIETIES REGISTRATION ACT XXI OF 1860

Registration No. S/ 1609/NE /~~2012~~ 2015

I hereby certify that DARYA. GANJ PATRI " SUNDAY BOOK BAZAR WELFARE ASSOCIATION

Located at Y-36, WELCOME SILAMPUR DELHI 110053

has been registered* under SOCIETIES REGISTRATION ACT OF 1860.

Give under my hand at Delhi on this 05th day of AUGUST Two Thousand ~~Twelve~~ Fifteen

Fee Rs. 50/- Paid

Seal

Registration of Societies

REGISTRAR OF SOCIETIES
GOVT. OF NCT OF DELHI
DELHI

* This document certifies registration under the Society Registration Act, 1860 However any Govt. department or any other association/ person may kindly make necessary verification (on their own) of the assets and liablities of the society before entering into any contract/assignment with them.)

Figure 8 Certificate of registration for 'Daryaganj Patri Sunday Book Bazaar Welfare Association' under the Societies Registration Act of XXI of 1860.

so on.[21] Despite two months of protests by the vendors, emphasising the historicity of the bazaar, its natural status, and the need for their presence on the streets, the authorities did not change their minds. The protests waned

[21] For time-lapse videos from the protest site, see Kanupriya Dhingra (2019), 'Delhi's Daryaganj second-hand books market: Going, going . . . but not quite gone yet?' *Scroll.in*. https://bit.ly/3KO2uOS.

Figure 9 Books being sold from inconspicuous spaces to avoid confiscation. (August 2019).

gradually and were eventually called off because of the Covid-19 pandemic.[22] The civic authorities regulated what they perceived as unregulated chaos in the bazaar, significantly changing how booksellers and book buyers could exercise spatialisation.

1.2 Mahila Haat: Relocation as Respatialisation

Daryaganj Patri Kitab Bazaar was sent off the streets and moved to Mahila Haat, a closed compound owned by the North Delhi Municipal Corporation of Delhi (NrDMC). The change of location entailed *respatialisation* of the Sunday Book Market. Some of the rhythms inside the new location for the book bazaar imitated the earlier rhythms pertinent to the bazaar's operation on the street, and others were new. The changes in rhythms of the book

---

[22] Kanupriya Dhingra (2020), Why the Lockdown and Physical Distancing Have All but Ended Delhi's Iconic Used Books Market.' *Scroll.in.*

Figure 10 Pamphlet designed by Chitra Chandrashekharan, a community artist who joined the booksellers in the protest for several weeks.

Figure 11 Protests on Netaji Subhash Marg. The poster reads, 'Save the girl child, educate the girl child; how will she study without books?' The book-sellers can be seen being interviewed by several journalists. Many regulars and locals recorded the protest on their phone cameras. (August 2019).

bazaar inside Mahila Haat predominantly relate to how the sellers and buyers occupied the new space. The relocation also implied a renegotiation of the degree to which chance and order came together for the second-hand book business in Old Delhi.

The relocation of the book bazaar was a directive towards modernisation. Netaji Subhash Marg and Asaf Ali Marg were among the roads whose spatial atmosphere has been utilised for commercial purposes historically and in the present, as is reflected in the aesthetic bearing of these streets. Book trade happened here via proper concrete shops and offices and via the informal setting of a makeshift bazaar. In fact, as discussed earlier, the impermanent Sunday Book Market played a key role in the establishment of more permanent brick-and-mortar bookstores in the area that imitated the

ways of the bazaar. While the 'formal' book business continues to thrive on
the streets of Netaji Subhash Marg and Asaf Ali Marg, it was the informal
bazaar that was removed and relocated. Mahila Haat is directly across from
Asaf Ali Marg, where part of the bazaar used to be before it was removed.
However, despite its proximity to the old site of the bazaar, the new Sunday
Book Market at Mahila Haat is further removed from its original 'historical'
and 'natural' location. Several buyers noted that the reaching Mahila Haat
was inconvenient since it faces traffic on the road from the opposite
direction; many couldn't even locate it without asking for directions.

Mahila Haat creates a different experience of book buying and selling,
despite its proximity to the streets where the original book bazaar flourished
for decades. Located above the New Delhi Municipal Corporation's multi-
level parking lot on Asaf Ali Marg, the original purpose of creating/
allotting this compound to the first Mahila Haat or Women's Mart in
Delhi in 2011 was to create a market space for women artisans across the
country to sell household items. The experiment was not a success, and the
relocation of the book vendors here in September 2019 is but the most recent
of such experiments by the civic body, following several failed attempts in
the past.[23] This may be because, in the previous experiments, the location of
Mahila Haat was not advertised properly. In the case of the booksellers, not
only did they advertise the location better with the help of print media,
online news, and social media, but they also attracted a portion of the
previous market's visitors. Banners were put across Netaji Subhash Marg
and Asaf Ali Marg to inform buyers who came looking for the Patri Kitab
Bazaar. The sense that I got from my interviews with the visitors at Mahila
Haat between September 2019 and February 2020 was that in the initial few
weeks, only regular buyers, such as students and *shauqeen* buyers
(Daryaganj connoisseurs) returned, and they had come to know about the

---

[23] The Mahila Haat at Asaf Ali Marg was marketed as the first of its kind to be set
up in Delhi in 2011, but no such *haats* were set up after it. See: The Haat to be
utilised for purposes other than the original, as North Delhi Municipal
Corporation became cash-strapped over time: Vibha Sharma, 'Mahila Haat,
Ramlila Ground may host weddings, private parties soon', *Hindustan Times*,
20 January 2017, New Delhi.

market via news reports or social media. The booksellers inside Mahila Haat helped me recognise some of the regulars. Student bodies from Delhi University colleges such as Maitreyi College, Kirori Mal College, Kamla Nehru, and Lady Shri Ram College for Women who had participated in the protests held between July and August 2019 also created awareness on social media after the relocation. Even as the regular book buyers, still found their way back to the vendors inside Mahila Haat, the *patri* booksellers lost the incidental readership, which had contributed to their business to a great extent. On the streets, the bookstalls attracted many pedestrians by chance. This incidental book buying contributed to the 'natural' status of the book bazaar, which helped prevent its relocation until September 2019.

1.2.1 Rhythms Inside Mahila Haat

Inside Mahila Haat, the essential routine of the Patri Kitab Bazaar gets repeated every Sunday. It is similar to the modes of trade exercised on the streets: buying books as one walks about the space and sees them laid out, the patterns of bargaining and negotiation, and so on. However, Mahila Haat is an independent space with its own rhythms. The serendipity of the streets, which played a significant role in the business, is restricted within the gated complex of Mahila Haat. In the Patri Kitab Bazaar, trade relied on incidental buying as much as it did on intentional visits and purchases. Any walker on those footpaths was a potential buyer. In the closed space of Mahila Haat, no one can *accidentally* become a book buyer, as was typically the case with Daryaganj Patri Kitab Bazaar.

Inside the Haat, the crowd is definite. Those who are present have decided to step inside the book market and buy books for their home libraries and their children or to prepare for their examinations, or to resell books for a profit at their bookstores. The gated architecture of the Haat has a different aesthetic and social appeal. The ambience inside Mahila Haat is rather slow and relaxed, unlike the active and dynamic space of the over-crowded streets, much like a Book Fair or a *pustak mela*. (Figure 15),[24]

---

[24] Delhi hosts two major annual book fairs: The Delhi Book Fair and The World Book Fair. In my understanding, the aesthetic and official arrangement of bookstalls in Mahila Haat, each Sunday, is much closer to that of these book

Inside the Haat, the floor is marked with where the booksellers should sit, leaving the remaining space for the book buyers to walk and explore. A buyer could maintain a slow pace, and there is no rush to hop onto the next stall, as was the case with the bazaar on the footpath where there was only so much space where one could walk, and the likelihood of being pushed around. Inside the Haat, it was easier to return to a stall since the crowd was limited and more engaged in a singular activity – buying books. At the bazaar, by contrast, people huddled at each bookstall as other readers joined, cutting across the queue of booksellers, until they were tired and left. As such, walkers could spatialise the book market through their movements and separate it from the other co-existing spaces and activities on the street, mapping the market with their footsteps amidst the various other occupations and places simultaneously present. Inside the Haat, with only the *book bazaaris* occupying a fixed space for set hours on a Sunday, the rhythm of the relocated book market is relatively isolated, unlike the polyrhythmic atmosphere on the streets. The space is predefined to establish a degree of order against the street's chaos. Mahila Haat has several places to sit, mull over your purchase, or meet your friends. Children play on the mowed grass inside the green spaces at Mahila Haat. The same chaiwallah visits periodically to serve tea to all the vendors and the few buyers. He dreams of having a tea stall inside the premises of the new book market one day, he tells me. In this way, stability creates dreams of mobility for some.

The relocation of the book market from the streets to the Haat has brought some notable changes in the bookselling strategies adopted by the vendors over the years. Mahila Haat has an 'entry gate' – a designated threshold – which makes the spatiality closer to that of a bookshop. While the booksellers still rely on serendipity and chance, since their stock still retains incoherence as compared to that of a proper bookshop, they have adapted new ways to maximise their visibility to the buyers and attract them

fairs. Apart from the local and international publishers at the book fair, a significant portion of the booksellers who set up their stalls in the two book fairs are vendors from the Patri Kitab Bazaar/Mahila Haat. Much like Mahila Haat, in the book fairs the sellers rent one (or more) stall(s) which have their dimensions and rent specified.

to their stall. Some older methods were retained. The book spines were stacked neatly, or the books were put in piles, with appealing chaos and the promise of a 'find' in the heap. However, some booksellers were seen to be experimenting with this new space: stall *sajana* (or setting up a stall) found new meanings, as sellers reinterpreted the available space and updated their knowledge of bookselling. As we see in Figure 12, one of the booksellers decided to arrange his stock by creating four walls out of books and standing inside the fort-like shape. In Figure 13, we see that Farid Anwar, who sells books for children, has brought in new features including book-stands, colourful sunshades, and low tables to house the books – also protecting them from water on the floor in the case of rain.

1.2.2 Order over Chaos

Unlike how serendipity dominated the experience of bookselling and buy-ing on the streets, order prevailed inside Mahila Haat, in various forms.

Figure 12 Fort-like arrangement of a bookstall inside Mahila Haat (October 2019).

Figure 13 'Glamorous' arrangement of a bookstall inside Mahila Haat (October 2019).

Mahila Haat is cleaner and more organised than the streets – which is one of the reasons why the officials at the NrDMC provided to persuade the booksellers in favour of this location. Other suggestions included the famous Ramlila Maidan and Hindi Park. The booksellers rejected these alternatives – and there were not many – because they were too far from the previous Patri Kitab Bazaar location and possibly because other commercial or non-commercial activities would have disrupted the sale of books. At Ramlila Maidan, for instance, another internal 'committee' works towards organising events. The vendors were worried they would have to go through another form of external regulation, which would affect their business and contrast with the limited autonomy they enjoyed on the streets, which came with internal modes of organisation by the vendors. Further, they were concerned that the alternatives of parks and *maidans* were not conducive to creating an experience of book vending similar to that offered by the streets, which was crucial. They saw footpaths as relatively more

Figure 14 Passive ambience inside Mahila Haat soon after the relocation. (September 2019).

dynamic than a *maidan* or a park. Similarly, not every footpath is likely to produce the same experience. Golcha Cinema was not the primary location for the Patri Kitab Bazaar. The bazaar saw some minor relocations – suggested by either the booksellers themselves or by the civic authorities. Netaji Subhash Marg and Asaf Ali Marg are both easily accessible commercial spaces. Daryaganj's location between New Delhi and Old Delhi made it convenient for various readers and book buyers from all over the city to visit the bazaar. The construction of a Delhi Metro station near Dilli Gate also brought in many new customers, while older customers could now visit more frequently.

Some of the vendors' fears came true inside Mahila Haat. The rent paid for one's stall immediately affected the sales and the selling patterns. Inside Mahila Haat, the vendors are asked to pay a fixed amount of rent – yet another form of regulation. The total weekly rent for the space is divided amongst the number of booksellers who set up their shop inside Mahila Haat

Figure 15 The Annual World Book Fair at Pragati Maidan, Delhi. Several
Daryaganj booksellers set up their stalls here, bringing more stock than in
the bazaar. (January 2020).

each Sunday. The rent is much higher than what the sellers paid earlier for
street squatting. Higher costs have affected the price at which the vendors
sell their books. The vendors took time to learn the 'types' of books in
demand at the new site. Some vendors at Mahila Haat who said they had to
accept the alternative after waiting for so long still hoped that the Daryaganj
Patri Kitab Bazaar would be restored to its former glory. For weeks,
business at Mahila Haat did not go well. Many booksellers also claimed it
was only feasible for them to bring smaller amounts of books to the Haat;
their godowns were further away now, and the space was limited and
relatively more expensive than the streets. On the streets, the ability to
spread books across the footpath worked in the vendor's favour, allowing
for titles to be visible to passers-by. This was no longer possible within the
six-by-four-foot space allocated per stall (unless the seller paid for more
than one block of space). The situation was worse for the booksellers who

set up their stalls towards the rear end of the complex as they did not get equal attention from visitors, who may have felt exhausted before making it to the far side of the complex.

The ease of locating bookstalls on the streets was pitted against the orderliness and beautification of Mahila Haat. Mahila Haat was the more 'modern' choice. It was likely to attract people who felt unsafe on the streets. 'Mahila Haat has a certain 'glamour' to it, but that doesn't necessarily help business', claimed several vendors. The 'glamour' is the book bazaar's beautified, sanitised, organised, orderly, and less chaotic form. In one of the 'orders' placed in the bazaar, the civic authorities have demanded that (i) *'Park mein cup, plate, glass, aadi daalna sakht mana hai'* ('Littering cups, plates, glasses, etc., is prohibited'); (ii) *'Park ke andar tent, sofa, chair daalna sakht mana hai'* ('Installing tents, sofa, and chairs inside the park is prohibited'); and (iii) *'Yeh plastic-mukt park hai'* ('This park is plastic-free'). The institutional regulation, orderliness, and organisation that differentiate the market inside Mahila Haat from the street bazaar were, in fact, what caused a loss of business for quite some time. Those who foresaw the constraints and were wary of the cost of setting up the market at Mahila Haat every week stopped coming to the market altogether and began to operate their businesses via phones and the internet. Hence, contrary to what the civic authorities had proposed, relocating the bazaar did not immediately or directly lead to a positive professional experience, even for a book bazaar that had been popular and beloved for several decades.

It's not as if the state prohibits using the streets for purposes other than walking. There are ways in which the periodic use of the streets is supported for cultural purposes – say, street art and exhibits or fairs. Further, periodic book markets are not a new phenomenon exclusive to Delhi. Temporary spaces for books on the streets do exist on the global map and in the Indian subcontinent. Kolkata's College Street or *Boi Para* (literally translated as Book Town) is the world's largest and one of the oldest book markets.[25] However, in the past few years the state government of Kolkata has proposed an ambitious, centralised book mall, which will cover an area as

---

[25] Diti Bhattacharya (2024), *Unfolding Spatial Movements in the Second-Hand Book Market in Kolkata: Notes on the Margins in the Boipara*, (Routledge).

large as all of the existing bookstores on College Street combined. However, booksellers are reluctant to move, and the city dwellers have reacted similarly to the relocation, claiming that the book market will lose its soul.[26] They agree, much like the Daryaganj booksellers, that the nostalgia associated with *Boi Para* also translates into business, and any additional 'glamour' would not be quite as profitable. Daryaganj Patri Kitab Bazaar is not nearly as old as College Street, which is said to have started in 1817. However, residents, migrants, and tourists have periodically occupied this street for five decades, and they have recounted the experience as authentic and carrying a unique flavour. Daryaganj Patri Kitab Bazaar was one of the ways to experience the city and its ever-changing character. Famous *shauqeen* visitors include author Khushwant Singh, historian Ramachandra Guha, oral historian Sohail Hashmi, and blogger Mayank Austen Soofi, known as *The Delhi Walla* – also the title of his blog.[27] There is also a vast number of online and offline reviews in the form of personal blogs and web and print articles that speak about this market, its uniqueness, and its place in the city. These buyers and Daryaganj enthusiasts have stepped up each time the bazaar has been endangered in the past, including the relocation in 2019. The resilience of *shauqeen* buyers such as Guha, Soofi, and Sohail Hashmi is a straightforward way of challenging authorities and their opinion that the chaos of unruly sites in the urban landscape must be organised and beautified. In this way, the buyers and the sellers wish to retain their status as active enablers of the street space.

The relocation of the book bazaar is indicative of the larger narrative of sanitisation and regulation – that is, attempts to regulate the ways to look at or experience the city. Urban anthropologist Sanjay Srivastava argues that defining or restricting the use of public space is a modern form of urban governance over everyday infrastructures. In *Entangled Urbanism: Slums, Gated Community and Shopping Mall in Delhi and Gurgaon*, he gives the example of the phenomenon of installing gates that create physically demarcated residential localities. Such 'gating' began in Delhi as early as the 1980s.

[26] From interviews conducted at College Street, Kolkata in 2020.
[27] See Ramachandra Guha (2018), 'Save the Daryaganj Book Bazaar, Once Again.', *Hindustan Times*.

Figure 16 Author Khushwant Singh declares his love for street book markets. Published in *Hindustan Times* on 31 December 2005 (photo source: Sumit Verma, a book vendor at Daryaganj).[28]

The raison d'être of installing gates is regulation of movement.[29] Confined spaces can be supervised more efficiently, unlike chaotic spaces such as streets. Srivastava's observation on gated complexes resonates with the spatial politics of relocating Daryaganj Patri Kitab Bazaar to a more regulated space.

[28] Singh recounts his experience of buying books from street markets across the world: London's Cambridge Circle, the Seine River outdoor booksellers in Paris, bookstalls around Mumbai's Flora Fountain, Kolkata's College Street, and Daryaganj Patri Kitab Bazaar. He addresses the corruption with which the police officials and the civic authorities at Municipality exploit the booksellers on the streets in Daryaganj.

[29] Sanjay Srivastava (2015), *Entangled Urbanism: Slum, Gated Community, and Shopping Mall in Delhi and Gurgaon* (Oxford University Press), pp. 113–114

Enacted by the civic authorities with minimum consideration of the book vendors' opinions or comments, the relocation was a way to bring in order and eliminate the chaos that the bazaar allegedly created on the streets.

The officials at NrDMC believe that Delhi has the potential to be a smart city, in which case order overrules chaos in making public spaces more user-friendly and exclusive. Displacing the book bazaar from the streets is a deliberate move towards building a modern, smart city by eliminating the older ways in which the space of the street has been operating. When I interviewed historian Sohail Hashmi – an acclaimed spokesperson for Delhi's past and present – in 2019, he passionately argued for a manner of regulation and institutionalisation that actually benefits the street vendors instead of relocating them from the streets. Street vending worked for the booksellers. However, if the traffic and encroachment-related concerns were sustained despite the level of regulation by the civic authorities, Hashmi suggests that the regulation could have been redirected towards, for instance, the navigation of traffic on Sundays alone. In other words, the idea of redevelopment, as adopted by the civic authorities, could have been balanced with a proposal related to reusing the streets to bring order into the same streets, such that the loss of serendipity is minimal. Yet, the possibility of chaos that disturbs the better functioning of other 'regular' rhythms of the same streets is decreased. 'How can any city that talks of being civilised discourage the sale of second-hand books?' argues Hashmi. 'It should be institutionalised by finding an alternative approach that would lead to a better, judicious "re-use" of the original site on the street itself.'

Delhi's hybrid architectural landscape hides several monuments among other markers of its historicity. You may discover them as you try to simply *be* in this city – much like finding books in the Sunday book market. Daryaganj Patri Kitab Bazaar happened to be a rather serendipitous institution (historical as it was) that the city would hide and unhide on Sundays. Those who knew of it would compulsively never skip a visit. Those who did not know of it would have – had they chanced upon the streets of Daryaganj. However, with the sterile repurposing of the streets allocated to the book market, that is not the case anymore. You may not accidentally become a book buyer as you once might have. It is all part of a larger plan now, and we may have lost the *original* Patri Kitab Bazaar to this plan.

1.3 Reflection: Space as Paratext

In *For Space*, Doreen Massey conceptualises space as a process: an indefinite, heterogeneous mix of chance and order. Massey states: 'What space gives us is simultaneous heterogeneity; it holds out the possibility of surprise; it is the condition of the social in the widest sense, and the delight and the challenge of that.'[30] If we understand space simply as a map, 'the assumption is precisely that there is no room for surprises'.[31] To spatialise, or, in this case, regularise the occupation of urban, open-ended spaces such as the Daryaganj Patri Kitab Bazaar, the civic authorities at the MCD attempted to avert surprises. That is, their move was directed towards increasing the ratio of 'order' versus chance and chaos. Following Massey's suggestion on this equation of order and chance in a given space, such an attempt goes a long way towards making a space more predictable, with minimum potential for resistance: 'In this representation of space, you never lose your way, are never surprised by an encounter with something unexpected, never face the unknown.'[32] By relocating the bazaar from the streets to a closed, rented space, the agency of locating and spatialising the book bazaar no longer belonged entirely to the vendors or the walkers. On the streets, the intersection of several rhythms simultaneously created the possibility of chance. As I have shown through several examples in this section, it is characteristic of the space of a street to *entail* surprises. The commercial, visual, and sensory experience of buying and selling books in Daryaganj Patri Kitab Bazaar happened because of this possibility of surprises, because of the serendipity that streets entail. Can we then say that this spatial serendipity fundamental to the streets is an essential component of the parallel communication circuit of books found in Daryaganj, like a paratextual component?

A paratextual element incorporated in a book is used to enhance its context, build interest around it, and influence the way a text is received.[33] Paratextual elements have a dual function: that of enhancing our understanding of whatever we make of a book, and also limiting it by creating

---

[30] Doreen Massey, *For Space* (SAGE, 2005), p. 105.

[31] Ibid, p. 111.

[32] Ibid, p. 111.

[33] Gerard Genette, *Paratexts: Thresholds of Interpretation* (Cambridge University Press, 1997), p. 1.

physical and intellectual boundaries in the form of interventions produced
by the authors or the publishers, in the form of covers, prefaces, indexes,
epilogues, appendices, and post-scripts, or even the interviews and reviews
that follow the publication of a book. In the context of a book traded at
Daryaganj, the space of the street operates in a related way. A book's
'location' on the streets both enhances and limits its definition. Unlike
a 'proper' bookshop where only 'new' books are sold, only *nayi-jaisi* (like
new) second-hand, used, and pirated books make their way to the bazaar.
Their physical condition, how the seller has procured them, and the value
that the seller and/or the buyer determine explain their placement on the
footpath. A book found on the footpath does not necessarily have to be
equated with discarded trash that has a degraded value because it has been
used more than once or because of how and where it was procured. On the
contrary, it is likely to become a valuable object of desire for a bibliophile,
a book collector, or anyone who associates the brittle object of an old book
with a memory or a quality that may not be found in the same book in
a 'proper' bookshop. For the buyer, a book's location on the footpath that
seems serendipitous and random, and the fact that an odd copy has been
'found' with the *kabadiwallah* (paper merchant) or on the footpath in
Daryaganj, becomes integral to the experience of procuring the book, and
then keeping or reading it. Hence, I argue that the parallel space of the *patri*
is strongly associated with, if not fundamental to, the books found in
Daryaganj. They are found in a part of Daryaganj periodically because
a parallel space has been created on the streets, allowing that presence.

   Daryaganj Patri Kitab Bazaar (and now Mahila Haat) has come to
represent a collective space for selling the books that *can* be found here. In
his study of footpath literature, *Passionate Modernity*, Srivastava argues that
footpaths are the site where subsets of cultural practices are formed as
a result of movements in tastes and fashions of contemporary capitalism as it
interacts with differing cultural traditions.[34] Srivastava's argument applies
to spaces where the street is utilised in a commercial capacity in urban India,
especially Delhi. Sarojini Nagar market, the largest flea market for apparels
in India, also embodies a similar flexible and makeshift aesthetic. Here, not

[34] Srivastava, *Passionate Modernity*, 175.

only are duplicate clothes and imported fabrics sold at low prices, but also a diverse range of fashion sensibilities co-exist. If we zoom out and look at the map of Delhi, we will find that Old Delhi has its own literary culture. Daryaganj Patri Kitab Bazaar is one of the components of this culture, the others being Urdu Bazaar near Jama Masjid, Chawri Bazaar as an old hub of 'dancing girls' and old poets such as Mirza Ghalib and Zauq, and later the hub of paper merchants, public libraries, and, not to forget, Nai Sarak. The literary culture that proliferates in this microgeography is unique in its own way. For instance, Nai Sarak near Chawri Bazaar metro station is a space for academic books that is open on weekdays and frequented by students, Urdu Bazaar with its stock primarily in one language. Daryaganj has become renowned for its sale of *nayi-jaisi* or 'parallel' books. These books encompass a wide range of genres and physical attributes, including imported fiction, encyclopedias, photocopied textbooks, budget guides, duplicate novels, pirated entertainment manuals, and more.

Further, the buyers and sellers of this bazaar embody specialised knowledge with which they have created their own parallel literary and commercial ecosystem of books at this site. As a result, the L-shaped footpaths of Netaji Subhash Marg and Asaf Ali Marg have been officially recognised as a 'natural' location for selling a specific variety of books. In fact, it is the largest centre for such books in the city, and the second largest in the country. Hence, it has been my point throughout this section that the books sold at this bazaar cannot be sold at the 'proper' places of circulation. The space of the street in Old Delhi was conducive to the book business that was operating in this location. For Mahila Haat to be as conducive, along with creating new patterns of occupation, sellers continue to abide by their knowledge of bookselling on the streets, as it has proven insightful for sixty years for the sale of parallel books of Daryaganj.

2 '*Hobby bhi hai, roti bhi*':
The Vendors of Sunday Book Bazaar

While interviewing the booksellers, I asked each of them the same question: *Aap meri kitab ke kirdar hain, mujhe apni kahani batayenge?* (You are a character in my book, would you like to share your story with me?) I pursued these stories as they were narrated to me. Most sellers invited me to sit with them on their side of the bookstall to listen patiently. (Amidst several anecdotes, there were also bits of poetry, stories of love and loss, and quite a lot of tea and snacks.) As a book buyer, I had hitherto always been on the other side of the footpath. By shifting to the booksellers' side, I experienced a shift in my gaze.

With a mix of participant observation and participant understanding, I could be a part of their experience. That is, I relied on both what they said and how they said it. The stories of the vendors are but novelistic elements that infiltrate the historical 'texts' that have tried, and often failed, to contain the bazaar. The ethnographic vignettes in this section will paint a picture of the vendors of the bazaar and elaborate on their complexities, paradoxes, contradictions, and the flexibility of their potential.

2.1 '*Ek* alag *Experience*': A Shared Rhetoric of Belonging

The book vendors at the Patri Kitab Bazaar associated '*garv*' (pride) and '*shauq*' (pleasure, interest, hobby) with their business, and frequently used these terms in their interviews. Often, they would talk about their '*lagaav*' (attachment) to the *patri* (pavement) and the business of selling books. They distinguish their community from other street vendors and street hawkers. While narrating their stories, they often found ways to communicate that their bazaar differed from other weekly or permanent street markets in Delhi and that selling books made it different. Selling books on the *patri* is not the same as selling everyday consumer goods found in most local weekly markets or LWMs (in official parlance), they implied.

All the Patri Kitab Bazaar vendors, whatever stock they may be selling, believe that books have a much higher value than any other consumer goods sold on the streets of Delhi. This is true especially for vendors specialising in the study-material circuit. They believed their profession

was contributing to the development and growth of education in Delhi –
something they were incredibly proud of. Puneet Kumar started selling
books at the Patri Kitab Bazaar in 1972, following a period of '*garibi*'
(poverty) and '*majboori*' (helplessness). He was one of the first vendors to
set up in the Patri Kitab Bazaar, and believes that only 'high quality'
students come to his stall, where he sells NCERT and CBSE textbooks
for much less than their original cost.[35] '*Mere ache relations hain in students se
jo Civils ke liye parhte hain, aur ab kuch toh IAS bhi ban gaye hain*' ('I have
good relations with the students who study for the civil services, and some
of them have become IAS officers as well'), he exclaims with pride.

  '*Hobby bhi hai, roti bhi*', said Asharfi Lal Verma about his business of
selling books on the *patri*: 'It is my hobby and my bread.' In a later
meeting, he exclaimed: '*Dekhiye, kuch kaam karne mein maza aata hai;
agar hum chahte to dukan ya naukri bhi kar sakte the. Lekin patri par kitab
bechna ek "alag" experience hai*' ('See, some professions give plain joy;
I could have done my business in a shop or gone for a salaried job. But
selling books on the *patri* is a "distinct" experience'). Asharfi Lal has
spent more than twenty years as a vendor in the Patri Kitab Bazaar. He
used to assist with selling books in a bookshop elsewhere in Delhi before
becoming a street vendor in Daryaganj. Rajesh Ojha, who sells a similar
stock of books in a rented shop on Netaji Subhash Marg, made this
enthusiastic and slightly exaggerated claim: '*Mere hisaab se is bazaar
mein kitaab bechne se achha kaam koi hai hi nahin. Ismein "enjoy" hai.
Aap jab kitaab chhantne lagte hain to time ka pata nahin chalta, bhookh-
pyaas nahin lagti, itna maza aata hai, oho!*' ('According to me, there is no
better profession than selling books in this bazaar. There is a lot of
"enjoy" [enjoyment] in this profession. You do not care about the time
you have spent sorting books; you can go hungry and thirsty; it is so
much fun, *aah!*'). Like Ojha, most of the vendors I talked to who
belonged to the traditional and study circuits spoke about the pleasure

---

[35] The NCERT (National Council of Educational Research and Training) is an
autonomous organisation of the government of India that assists the central and
state governments on policies and programmes related to school education.
CBSE refers to the Central Board of Secondary Education.

they derive from sorting (i.e. putting their knowledge to work). Sorting books, in fact, is key to bookselling at the Patri Kitab Bazaar. The books of Daryaganj are drawn from various parallel sources, such as paper markets; discarded stock from public, private, and individual libraries; remainder stock from publishers; and so forth. Booksellers derive pleasure and enjoyment from creating value out of books derived from these parallel sources. Their pleasure is linked to how they perform and choose to specialise in this business. That contrasts with vendors (who I later address as 'detached' or those who feel less *lagaav* with the book business at Daryaganj), such as A. R. Khan and Manmohan Singh, who suffer from greater financial instability. However, despite the insecurity and lack of profits, they have been part of this community for a long time, showing that this bazaar has space for both specialised and non-specialised sellers.

Related stories followed from almost all the vendors I interviewed. There was one common thread, however, with each vendor describing how selling books at Daryaganj is what Asharfi Lal calls *alag* or distinct: just as the market is officially regarded as a specialised weekly bazaar compared to other local weekly markets, the vendors too believe that their profession is specialised and more sophisticated than it may appear because of its location and operation on a *patri* in Old Delhi.

Let me introduce you to the booksellers who have actualised Daryaganj Sunday Book Market over the years, and how they 'arrived' here.

2.2 Trajectories into the Bazaar

2.2.1 Via Family and *Ustads*

For the vendors of Daryaganj, family and networks of kinship are the most common routes into the book trade. The seven famous Kumar brothers are an excellent example of this. Their father introduced them to the basic principles of hawking and bookselling. After selling books at different sites in the city – mostly pavements, bus stands, and railway stations – they discovered Daryaganj as one of the areas where bookselling could be pursued rather stably. Each of them has been in this business since they started working at an early age, and the two elder-most brothers are among the few vendors who had established the *patri* business from its days around Subhash Park.[36] Vendors continue to bring their family members into the business.

The second typical trajectory the vendors follow to enter this profession is through mentors and intermediaries. Fifty-seven-year-old Mahesh has spent thirty-five years as a bookseller at Daryaganj Sunday Book Market. His brother was in the business before him, but not at the Patri Kitab Bazaar. However, both brothers were trained by someone he refers to as their *ustad* (mentor/trainer). Mahesh informed me that his ustad had also trained other men. When Mahesh started, only a handful of second-hand book vendors operated at this site; the business has grown in the past two decades. While Mahesh has been able to earn a livelihood solely from selling books at the bazaar, unlike most vendors in the bazaar he is determined not to bring his children into the business. He would prefer salaried jobs for them. Like many vendors, Mahesh also senses that the book business in Daryaganj has no future because digital books and digital marketplaces will take over: '*internet par hi bikengi kitabein*', he says – 'Books will only sell on the internet'.

2.2.2 From One Profession to Another

Family and mentors are not the only traditional ways to enter this profession. Divakar Pandey's brothers signed up for the Indian army, but he could not pass the medical tests to be eligible to sit for the main examination. In his case, his profession became an exception in his family. However, Pandey didn't immediately begin selling books at the Patri Kitab Bazaar. Before he started his business at Daryaganj, he worked for A. H. Wheeler in Rajasthan.[37] He later moved to Delhi to work as a sales assistant for DK

---

[36] Subhash Park is where the first signs of the Patri Kitab Bazaar started to appear before its sixty-year run on the pavements of Netaji Subhash Marg and Asaf Ali Marg and its recent relocation to Mahila Haat.

[37] Set up by Emile Edouard Moreau, A. H. Wheeler & Co. Pvt. Ltd. (commonly known as 'A. H. Wheeler', or 'Wheeler') was a chain of railway bookstalls, operating since 1877, and the oldest in the field. Their operation shut down in 2018.

Publishing and Prakash Publications, located in the nearby Ansari Road. In fact, most booksellers at Daryaganj Sunday Patri Kitab Bazaar have engaged with the book business in more than one way, and some of them continue to do so, which either compensates or supplements bookselling at the bazaar.

Other vendors also navigated several professions before settling in Daryaganj. Ashok has been a bookseller at the bazaar for twenty-five years. Born into an underprivileged family in East Delhi, Ashok raised money for his family and his education through petty jobs such as pulling a rickshaw and hawking. After earning his bachelor's degree in commerce from Delhi University's Ram Lal Anand College, Ashok joined the New Delhi Municipal Corporation. However, he continued with other businesses, too, for a while, seeking ways to increase his income. Bookselling was only one of his several jobs, until it became a permanent professional pursuit. '*Main sangharsh karta tha, kitabon ke zariye kuch bana. Chaar baje uthta tha, newspaper daalta tha, office jata tha, lunch mein magazine aur kitabein bechta tha — aadmi ko samay ke anusar parivartan karna padta hai*' ('I used to work hard. Selling books gave me an identity. I used to wake up at 4 am, sell newspapers, go to the office later, and sell books during lunchtime. A man must change with the demands of the time.')

Bookselling's capacity to reap profits and provide them with professional stability in the longer run made quite a few booksellers stay. Surendra Dhawan is an example. He turned his full-time profession as a freelance photographer into a part-time one and his part-time engagement with books into a full-time business. He told me about his transition from photographer to bookseller: photography was an exciting life that demanded different skills and constant movement across states and, at times, countries. He claims to have photographed Indira Gandhi, the former prime minister of India. It's his favourite memory from the profession. Several such remnants of his previous professional life were evident in his excitement during the discussion (he was always keen about the camera I was using and advised me on improving my photography). I was sceptical. How is pursuing photography less lucrative for a person who clicked photographs of the prime minister than selling books at Daryaganj?

Dhawan replied that his *shauq* (interest, pleasure) lies in photography still, but it was not a sustainable living. Working as a photographer entailed an erratic routine spread over unusual places countrywide. He said he needed to stay in one place in the longer run: '*Ab grahasthi bhi sambhalni hoti hai*' – his family required his presence. Even though bookselling might not be as thrilling an experience as photography, he opted for bookselling because he saw this as a sustainable profession. Much like Ashok, Dhawan had already begun investing in the used book business on the side, and he could see himself making that into a permanent option that could work for him.[38] A part of achieving this stability comes from a continuing familiarity with the mechanisms with which vendors operate within this bazaar.

2.2.3 '*Main Dilli se hoon*'

When I asked Sharif Ahmed, one of the senior Daryaganj vendors, how he arrived at the Patri Kitab Bazaar, his response was a shrug and these words: '*Main Dilli se hoon. Mujhe Daryaganj ke baare mein nahin pata hoga?*' ('I belong to Delhi. How would I have not known about Daryaganj?'), implying that for *Dilliwallahs*, knowledge about Daryaganj as a potential place of business has been rather obvious.

However, not all booksellers at the Patri Kitab Bazaar are *Dilliwallahs* (those who belong to Delhi). Migration is a common experience shared by many booksellers of Daryaganj. Hari Narayan Giri has been in the book-selling business for some twenty years. His father was a farmer, he tells me. Giri moved to the city from Ballia in Uttar Pradesh (approximately 280 kilometres from Delhi) to look for a job and found his way to the Patri Kitab Bazaar through 'contacts', he says. About his life as a bookseller, he feels '*yeh bahot behtar hai*' ('that this is far better than farming'). This is also a profitable and more stable business. Giri says that this has since become his way of life. Throughout the week, he collects books and sells them on Sundays – most of his stock comes from the paper market, where he buys discarded books for Rs. 40 per kilogramme. '*Double se bhi zyada margin hai*'

---

[38] Dhawan moved his business to a bookshop on Netaji Subhash Marg in early 2023, selling a similar stock of second-hand books for a 'fixed price'. He doesn't have to maintain a warehouse.

('The profit margin is more than double'), he tells me. Giri is one of the innumerable migrants who, leaving their familial and social networks, came to the city and settled for a sense of 'permanent ephemerality'.[39] In fact, more than half the booksellers I interviewed said that city jobs were more financially rewarding than farming.

These migrants may be highly educated or *anparh* (illiterate), and none of them had prior knowledge about bookselling at the Patri Kitab Bazaar. As much as their lives as migrants are affected by macroeconomic forces, I identify the booksellers of Daryaganj as enablers of the urbanisation of the streets of Old Delhi. On departing from their primary/traditional occupational roots and becoming a bookseller 'by chance', as they often exclaimed, they applied their own economic strategies in the given urban milieu, providing them with the stability they desired from the city. The booksellers of Daryaganj – both migrants and natives of Delhi – have collectively 'created' and enabled the Patri Kitab Bazaar by incorporating complex, specialised knowledge of selling books on the streets. In this way, the vendors are not an 'excluded', 'marginalised', or 'surplus population' but aspirational dwellers in the immanent pursuit of opportunities.[40] Hence, the lives of the booksellers at Daryaganj are an example of how new forms of citizenship are formed in the urban space.

2.3 Specialising as a Pavement Bookseller

The vendors of the Patri Kitab Bazaar build unique bodies of knowledge which help them in their business. These knowledge corpora comprise information about sourcing books, choosing a range of books for their stalls, acknowledging the evolving needs and tastes of buyers who visit the bazaar, value creation, and leveraging a viable profit margin. That is, it is a more complex process than simply coming to the bazaar and setting up a stall. For that matter, even how a vendor arranges their stall constitutes part of this unique knowledge corpus. In Darnton's proper communication circuit, booksellers communicate with publishers, investors, and distributors, and vice

---

[39] Srivastava, p. 169.

[40] Veronica Gago (2018), 'What are popular economies?: Some reflections from Argentina', *Radical Philosophy*, pp. 32–38.

versa, to create databases about which books can be sold and how – which leads to generating a profit and facilitating said proper circuit.[41] In the Patri Kitab Bazaar, vendors have a limited supply and limited choice even if they choose/sort from their sources. That is, the act of sorting books, as it forms the basis of the business at the Patri Kitab Bazaar, is different from getting books from a distributor. Moreover, no ancillary marketing activities, such as book reviews and promotions, help a vendor at the Patri Kitab Bazaar. Vendors are on their own within each 'parallel' circuit of the bazaar – the traditional, study-material circuit, or that of 'D' books. The vendors' mutual creation of knowledge and updating it as and when there is a new source of books or new categories of book buyers in the market keep their businesses at the Patri Kitab Bazaar running. Hence, instead of official mechanisms, databases, or literary agents and reviews, customers and the sources from which their books arrive are the enforcers of business.

2.3.1 Choosing and Building 'Knowledge Corpora'

One of the simplest ways to classify the vendors at the Patri Kitab Bazaar is by looking at the type or genre of books they sell. During my fieldwork, I noticed that a few vendors chose not to demonstrate any specialisation; however, they constituted only a small fraction of the sellers. There are three principal 'circuits' of books within which most vendors at the bazaar operate their business: the traditional circuit, the study-material circuit, and the circuit of 'D' books. In the 'traditional circuit', vendors sell second-hand books. Within this, some specialise in a specific language (Hindi, English, Urdu) or genre (art books, non-fiction, novels). Some vendors sell only novels in English. Within the 'study-material circuit', vendors sell current syllabus and/or out-of-syllabus books. The former includes coursebooks for schools, such as NCERTs or guidebooks for competitive exams. Some sell *kunjis* – small, inexpensive, plagiarised study guides with the latest content for specific courses and examinations of the local universities and institutions. 'Out-of-syllabus' books are relevant as extra-study material. These are adjacent to the school or university syllabi or for general

---

[41] Robert Darnton (1982), 'What is the History of Books?' *Daedalus* 111, no. 3: 65–83.

awareness. The circuit of piracy (what vendors call 'D *ki kitab*' or 'D Books') is independent and is available in two ways in the bazaar: local, plagiarised quasi-legal literature in the form of pocketbooks on topics such as self-help, entertainment, general knowledge, and so forth, or pirated copies of latest bestseller novels and self-help books.

Even though books from all three circuits were available in the market in the starting years of the bazaar – educational books from the import lot, and pirated pocketbooks from local publishers/printers – the first (traditional) circuit populated the market the most in its first decade, with at least 90 per cent of the vendors selling used novels, old magazines, and educational books, the majority of which were sourced from the *kabadiwallas* (paper/scrap dealers). Gradually, as the availability of and demand for study material increased, the number of vendors dealing exclusively in this circuit increased, and it became an independent circuit. Later, as piracy became widespread in the Indian publishing and circulation scene in the last decade, 'D *ki kitab*' became more visible in the market. Hence, almost all new book vendors sell pirated books. Most traditional vendors started by selling general/miscellaneous books and made their way to curating a bookstall with specialised books. What is relevant here is *how* the vendors become a part of these circuits and decided to specialise. The kind of sources and knowledge the vendors could/can access is the first consideration.

Let us look at Abdul Wali's journey into this profession, which will give us a glimpse into how a vendor 'arrives' at the Patri Kitab Bazaar, gains knowledge, and makes decisions related to what circuit they want to continue in.

Around 1972, Parvez Kumar Rohilla was popular among the vendors of the Patri Kitab Bazaar for the effort he would put into collecting and curating individual 'sheets', extracted from fashion and beauty magazines, both imported and local. Wali remarked: '*Professional aadmi the. Farrate se angrezi bolte the. Har Sunday red tie lagake aate the*' ('He was a professional. Used to speak English fluently. Wore a red tie every Sunday'). He would go around the city all days of the week to middlemen (intermediaries) and houses around the city to collect the primary material from which he would make 'files' (folders) of such sheets. He would sell a single sheet of fashion designs at a fixed price of Rs. 4 for the Western content and Rs. 2 for Indian content. These books were originally priced at Rs. 300–400, which was quite expensive for students. Buying only relevant pages for a much lower price, instead of the whole text that may not be useful in its entirety, was a better option. He also sold old editions of magazines such as *India Today* and *TIME* magazine. Wali still has these 'files' and a good collection of these magazines, but he doesn't sell them. There are no 'current buyers', says Wali. However, he is willing to wait for the right *shauqeen* buyer (Daryaganj afficionados), who would buy them from him at a higher value. Rohilla introduced Wali to the book business at Patri Kitab Bazaar. When he decided to quit, Rohilla asked Wali to acquire his stock. (Rohilla later started a matrimonial webpage, which, according to Wali, is doing quite well and gives Rohilla some much-needed rest.) However, Wali wasn't quite willing; he found Rohilla's mode of business exhausting and quite demanding. Hence, instead of dealing with fashion and beauty catalogues and old magazines, Wali entered the 'study-material circuit' to avoid 'hard work': '*Mehnat se bachne ke liye maine school line pakdi.*'

Forty-two-year-old Abdul Wali now runs a bookstore in West Badarpur, Delhi-53, and his principal source of income is his stall and the clientele at the Patri Kitab Bazaar. Before entering the book business, Wali tried to study for the civil service entrance exams. He also studied Arabic at the Modern Indian Languages Department at the Arts Faculty, University of Delhi – he was told there was good demand for Arabic teachers in the Gulf countries. However, he realised that there was too much competition. Further, his poor financial situation prevented him from delaying the search for a steady source of income. Wali's cautious yet strategic entrepreneurial attitude towards earning his livelihood in the early stages of his professional career extends towards how he pursues his business in the present day. He is not one to take risks:

> *Gautampuri, Seelampuri ke transport auction mein 100 rupaye kilo se boli shuru hoti hai. Samaaan katton mein band hota hai. Zyada maal lene waalon ko zyada discount milta hai. 40 rupaye kilo tak bhi mil jaata hai. Qamar bhai risk lete hain bade-bade. Import containers aate hain, to auction mein yeh sara maal khareed lete hain. Yeh wahaan ke king hain. Isliye inhein*

*discount bhi zyada milta hai. Main yeh nahin karta. Main
kitabein chant-ta hoon. 100–200 rupaye kilo mein, matlab ka
saamaan leta hoon. Zaroori hai! Maan lo, maine medical ki
kitab ka stock le liya; hai to wo bhi study-material, par mujhe
editions ki knowledge nahin hai na. Purana hua, to mera
nuksaan hai. Mujhe college ke study material ki 'special'
knowledge hai shuru se. To main wahi leta hoon. Bilkul risk
nahin leta. Hum auction se isiliye kam lete hain, kabadi se
zyada. Risk aur nuksaan dono kam hai, mehnat bhi. Qamar ji
ke paas bade godown hain, mere paas nahin hai. Bahot rent hota
hai. Main utna hi stock khareed-ta hoon jitna mujhse sambhala
jaye. Yahaan clients banata hoon. Ek student ko achha maal do,
wo agle saal phir aata hai, apne doston ke saath. Aise hi mera
business achha chal raha hai.*

The bid (for imported books) starts at Rs. 100 at the
transport auctions held at Gautampuri and Seelampuri. The
stock is packed in sacks. Those who buy more get a discount
(on the initial principal bidding amount). You can get it for
as little as Rs. 40 per kilo. Qamar bhai takes many risks. He
buys the whole stock in the auction whenever the import
containers arrive. He is considered a 'king'. That is why he
gets the biggest discounts too. I don't do this. I sort books.
I buy select stock at the price of Rs. 100 to Rs. 200 per kilo. It
is somewhat necessary! For instance, if I buy a stock of
medical books, which is also 'study material', I don't have
the required specialised knowledge of editions and content.
If the material is old, it will cause me loss. I have always
worked with the study material that is relevant to colleges.
So, that is what I buy. I don't take risks, so I buy less from
auctions and more from paper merchants. Along with less
risk and loss of profits, less hard work and labour are
involved. Qamar ji has huge storage units; I don't. I only
buy whatever I can store. I build my clientele here instead. If
you sell good, useful material to one student, they come

back the next year, along with their friends. This is how my
business has been running well.

Hence, Wali's escape from 'a lot of hard work' doesn't mean his business is
easy-going. It took skill, management, and knowledge to build the stock
and the clientele that he now has. He has his own mechanisms for acquiring
books. At the same time, he knows how to limit his stock: he doesn't try to
get into unnecessary competition with older vendors who also have more
experience and bigger spaces where they can store books. Further, even
within the study-material circuit, he has limited himself to a certain kind of
study material: he started his business by selling schoolbooks but has shifted
to selling low-priced guidebooks or *kunjis* and second-hand coursebooks
for the students of Delhi University and Jamia Millia Islamia. He avoids
buying any and every form of course material: he mentions medical books
as a particular exception since this involves extensive knowledge of relevant
editions and familiarity with the needs of a specific community of students.[42]
He tells me that there is also enough competition in his line of business. As
soon as the vendors of this circuit get information on any second-hand stock
availability at a paper market or with any individual *kabadiwallah*, they rush
to acquire it: '*Wo bees minute kehta hai to hum das minute mein pahonch jaate
hain*' ('If [the paper merchant] says twenty minutes, we get there in ten
minutes'). In the present day, a scrap dealer buys his stock from houses and
private and public libraries at a rate of Rs. 8–10 per kilo or for free at times.
Booksellers sort useful material from the scrap and buy it from the scrap
dealers at around Rs. 40 per kilo: ('*Jab maine business shuru kiya tha, tab
parents koi bhi books le lete the. R. D. Sharma chahiye hogi, to Manjit Singh bhi
chal jaati thi. Ab school chabi bharta hai. R. D. Sharma boli hai to wahi lenge*'
('Around the time I started my business [as a vendor of school books],
parents would buy any editions. They won't mind a *Manjit Singh* or an *R.D.
Sharma* [authors of popular companion books on mathematics]. Now, the

---

[42] Shyam Kishore is the only vendor at the Patri Kitab Bazaar who specialises in
medical books. He buys books directly from the publishers and sells them at
a discounted rate of 50 per cent of the original price. His stock includes books on
MBBS, nursing, and dental courses.

schools tell the students what to buy. If they've been asked to buy an R. D. Sharma, they'll not buy anything else').

2.3.2 '*Patri Ne Sikhaya*': Circumstantial and Experiential Knowledge

The diversity of sources and the active methods used to acquire books are key factors that influence vendors in determining their specialisation. At the point in the chronology of the bazaar's history at which a vendor joins the Patri Kitab Bazaar, diverse sources are being sought by the existing vendors. Even when the first few vendors decided to sell books at Daryaganj, they had fixed sources they could rely on: imported second-hand books, paper markets, private collections, libraries, and railway auctions. Magazines and novels were among the first 'books' to arrive at this *patri*. Since then, the books that the vendors of Daryaganj sell have arrived from alternative sources, and not in the ways that 'proper' vendors acquire books to be sold in their bookshops. Selling books at the Patri Kitab Bazaar is a crossover between street vending and proper bookselling. That is, not only does the vendor have to know how to sell books and have a sense of the 'commodity' they are selling, they also need to be aware of the ways in which bazaars operate. It's not a profession per se: you don't study to become a street vendor, therefore it's not an obvious career choice. However, there is training required.

The seven Kumar brothers are all in the same business, but each deals with a different genre of books. Having started with general books, they each specialised their stock over time: medical books, art books, syllabus books, novels, or books for competitive exams. This also allows the brothers to keep their businesses separate from each other. Further, their decision to diversify their businesses into different circuits can be considered a strategic move. They can reinforce certain power dynamics and hierarchy in the market by absorbing and producing knowledge of most of the mechanisms that have governed the bazaar.

The Kumar brothers now also have a bookshop and a printing press in Nai Sarak, where they repair some second-hand books to sell at the bazaar. Their extended book business is rooted in the experience at the Patri Kitab Bazaar: '*Ye bahot purani baatein hain*' ('These are very old matters'), says

Sushil Kumar, recounting the *purane din*, old days. Out of the seven brothers, Sushil Kumar was the first one to start selling books: '*Sabse pehle maine hi yahaan kitab bechna shuru kiya. Ek aane ki ek kitab bechte the. Jahaan khali jagah dikhti thi, waheen baith jaate the*' ('I was the first one to start selling books here. I used to sell one book for a penny. I would sit down wherever I found an empty space'). Initially, he would sell books for one anna (6.25 *paise*) each. In those days, vendors would sit anywhere they liked since there were not so many of them, and there was no need for external or internal regulation. Their father bought stocks of books, and the brothers were supposed to sell them. Over the years that followed, they began travelling across the country to gather books – something that quite a few booksellers do not do, as they depend on local sources.

Bookseller Niyazuddin tells me that he has never moved away from the traditional sources: local libraries and private collections. He travels either on public transport or on his scooter. As a result, his collection is not specialised since he has not put in the effort to curate or define a collection. He sells whatever he gets. Even though he started around the same time as Sushil Kumar, he remained modest about how he wanted to operate in the bazaar. Niyazuddin's case is an important exception – unlike what we have seen with the Kumar brothers or Abdul Wali, specialisation is not a necessary condition that defines the present-day traditional vendor.

The way a vendor acquired their training, combined with how they started their business at the bazaar and decided to lead the business in the future, is one way to classify the vendors of Daryaganj. Mahesh, whom we met earlier, started with miscellaneous stock based on whatever was available. He now sells books for competitive exams: IELTS, TOEFL, GRE, GMAT, and so forth. Mahesh's knowledge of bookselling is only partially due to the training he received from his *ustad*; the rest is from his experience on these streets – that is, a combination of training and circumstantial knowledge, as is true for various older vendors. Mahesh tells me '*Main bahot saari bhasha parh leta hoon. Bol nahin sakta, par dekh kar yeh bata dunga ke yeh kaunsi bhasha hai*' ('I can read multiple languages. I cannot speak in those many languages, but I can identify which language it is just by looking at it'). When I asked what languages he can read fluently, he told me he understands Dutch, German, Sanskrit, Spanish, and what he calls 'American'. Mahesh justifies his claim to be a polyglot based on his profession: '*Patri se sikha hai, madam*' ('I learnt it on the streets, Madam'). I asked him how: '*Anparh ko angrez ke beech mein chhor do wo bhi angrezi bolega*' ('Leave an illiterate amidst English-speaking people, and he will speak in English'). With time, Mahesh gained familiarity with his stock, and, corresponding to the demand for books, his 'knowledge' about his commodity increased. Students asked him about titles in different languages. By comparing those titles with his own, he figured out how to tell which language they were in. Like several of the vendors, Mahesh doesn't read the books he sells or has meagre information about their literary value: the value of books, for Mahesh, is limited to their titles, language, and how often his customers demand them. Those who followed Mahesh into the profession then adopted these skills. His knowledge, gained from a combination of training, experience, and chance, has become part of an informal, unofficial, and important repertoire for a new vendor who wants to sell the same stock. This is how Mahesh belongs to what I understand as the traditional community of vendors at Daryaganj Sunday Book Market. Each of these vendor's trajectories, then, demonstrates how the parallel business of book vending at the bazaar is related to the subsistence economy. It is informal, unprotected, and involves more risks than the 'proper' bookselling business.

2.3.3 '*Apna kaam toh apna kaam hi hai*':
Separating the 'Proper' from the 'Parallel'

Some vendors at the Patri Kitab Bazaar are also associated with the proper communication circuit: they help in bookshops or they have their own publishing and/or printing units. Specialising at the Patri Kitab Bazaar means that they distinguish between both experiences – the parallel and the proper – since they are not the same: the variety of books and the mechanisms adopted to sell them vary. I will show, with a few examples, how they differ.

Swastik Dogra's case challenges the notion that the booksellers of Patri Kitab Bazaar can benefit from the experience of selling books elsewhere and use that experience at the *patri*, and vice versa. As an assistant at Vijaykumar

Govindram Hasanand (a bookshop in Nai Sarak) on weekdays, he sells the available stock and assists in data entry. This is how he earns his fixed monthly salary. He says that he likes selling spiritual books, which the bookshop primarily stocks and sells. However, his agency there is limited. As a vendor at the Patri Kitab Bazaar, he sells books other than those on spirituality: novels, comics, and syllabus books for schools and colleges in Delhi, because this is what sells here and allows him a good profit margin. Dogra's case shows that the forms of self-management that the booksellers of Daryaganj Patri Kitab Bazaar acquire are combined with an ardent desire for autonomy. Dogra expresses it as such: '*Apna kaam toh apna kaam hi hai*' – He prefers selling books on the footpath, he says, because he owns this business. Dogra enjoys being a seller on the footpath instead of merely being a mediator in the bookshop where, more recently, he has mostly been managing their online catalogue. At the bazaar, Dogra is the boss. It is different from doing a day job at a bookshop or even owning one – a narrative repeated by several booksellers at the bazaar.

S. Chaudhry runs a successful book business on the nearby Ansari Road, called Masooma & Co, where he publishes and sells Urdu literature and textbooks. His customer base at the Patri Kitab Bazaar is quite different. However, at the bazaar, he sells his books at a discount of 40 per cent (unlike the 25 per cent discount at his shop), allowing students and Urdu literature readers to flock over to his bookstall. For instance, Chaudhry showed me a five-volume set of a much-requested *Urdu–English Dictionary*, which he sells at the Patri Kitab Bazaar for Rs. 2,000; at his shop, he sells it for Rs. 5,000. Thus, Chaudhry considers his buyers and their spending capacity while ensuring he doesn't lose money. (I later found the same five-volume set at another bookstall, on the same evening, being sold for Rs. 1,500 – and that, too, was before any negotiations.) Moreover, only a few bookstalls sell Urdu books in the Patri Kitab Bazaar, giving an edge to Chaudhary's stall. In both these cases – of Dogra and of Chaudhry – where booksellers either sell books at proper bookshops and at the *patri*, or when they both publish and sell books at more than one site, the Patri Kitab Bazaar may act as an additional, symbiotic site. However, bookselling at *patri* has its own parallel methods and knowledge, which the vendors must acquaint themselves with to make it a permanent profession.

2.3.4 Degree and Range of Specialisation

Even though there are many ways of becoming a bookseller at the Patri
Kitab Bazaar, vendors decide on their extent and range of professional
engagement with the books and the bazaar. Patri bookseller Manish specialises in antique books, which he then sells at book fairs and to an
exclusive customer base that he has developed over the years. He showed
me which kinds of books qualify as antique: first publications, association
books, signed copies, rare book covers, and so forth. These are some of the
titles he boasted of offering: an 1887 copy of *Gebir, Count and Julian* by
W. S. Landor, acquired from London (second-hand, UK containers);
a book from the library of Indraprastha Hindu Girls High School and
Interim College, last borrowed on '24.5.1925' by Radha, acquired from an
unidentified seller who bought it second-hand from another used book
market; a pocketbook of Greek art, *Gods and Goddesses in Art and Legend*,
published in 1950, acquired from a local 'contact'; and some 1977 editions of
Women's Era magazine and 1974 editions of *Reader's Digest*, both acquired
from a local reader's private collection, on their demise, when sold by their
family members. How did he achieve this quite specialised knowledge? He
explained that there was no one way to find a collection of such books – he
must be on the constant lookout. Over the years, he had identified reliable
sources in Delhi and looked for similar contacts outside the city. Some
intermediaries stock such rare books but, according to Manish, that is
a more expensive option. He doesn't approach the intemediaries unless it
is to acquire a 'special' book. One of the ways for him to acquire an
affordable collection with which he can maximise his profits is to rely on
other booksellers' stocks. One of his preferred stalls is that of Bheem, who
also has a collection of such books and brings some of his stock every
Sunday. Bheem sells them to his customers for as little as Rs. 50 without
worrying much about how rare the book may be. The stock is even cheaper
for Bheem because he buys in bulk. He exclaims that, unlike Manish, he isn't
as interested in growing his business. Bheem seems content with selling
books as they reach him. *Patri* business offers him basic stability and
security – and that is all he seeks. Manish is more entrepreneurial and
exploits the knowledge he has accumulated. The symbiotic professional

relationship between Manish and Bheem reflects how a particular aspect of business operated in the Patri Kitab Bazaar. In the early hours of setting up the market every Sunday, quite a few booksellers would take rounds of other bookstalls, looking for titles they think would fetch a better price.

A vendor at the Patri Kitab Bazaar needs familiarity with the materiality of a book beyond its content: covers, paratextual paraphernalia, the oldness or newness of a book, the marginalia (such as the signatures and their relevance to a buyer), why only specific books are requested repeatedly and if those books can be stocked again, and so on. While this may be similar to how vendors at other second-hand book markets acquire their knowledge, the booksellers of these markets are situated or 'located' uniquely. As much as the city and the street where they sell books are different, so too are their individual life histories and entrepreneurial contexts. Hence, the biography of a book bazaar is formed with the help of the biography of the booksellers who, by being situated here, have helped in locating the book market.

This profession requires situated knowledge, or how the vendors acquire and appropriate what Veronica Gago calls 'forms of doing and knowing', about the business of selling books at this location, with the used/pirated books as their saleable commodity.[43] The kind of knowledge this business requires is also different from the business of proper bookselling. Since they don't read the books, and there are no formal mechanisms which could provide them with an estimate of the value of the books, either literary or commercial – something that proper booksellers gain from understanding the latest publishing and sales patterns – there are specialised means for them to acquire the forms of knowledge that are required to be able to find stability in this business. The sellers, especially those who have formed specialised circuits, must know the books they sell. The booksellers at the Patri Kitab Bazaar require familiarity with the buyers' needs. Pricing books is based on a quick evaluation: a balance between their knowledge of the 'value' of the stock and an analysis of what the buyer wants/can afford to pay. These are ways to make these sellers a community 'parallel' to that of proper booksellers and regular street vendors selling other commodities.

[43] Gago, 31.

This is one of the reasons why, as discussed in the previous section, Daryaganj Sunday Book Market is officially recognised as a specialised market.

2.3.5 In the Absence of '*Shauq*'

Vendors, despite having similar training and similar stock of books, may have different degrees of interest in the business. A. R. Khan didn't receive any training. Further, luck didn't favour him much. The promise of stability I noted in Ashok Kumar's and Surendra Dhawan's cases has remained unfulfilled in A. R. Khan's case, who started in this business in 1985. His father-in-law suggested that he sell the novels in Hindi and Urdu that he had hoarded in his house to earn some extra money, which is how his journey as a bookseller in Daryaganj began. He left vending between 2009 and 2017. Before he moved to Mahila Haat, he used to sell books near the Daryaganj branch of the Bank of Baroda, located on Asaf Ali Marg. However, it has never been his primary means of a livelihood. Khan is a retired teacher of Urdu in a government school, where he taught for twenty-seven years. He was a scriptwriter at his institution's radio programme for a few years and is quite invested in Urdu and Hindustani as literary languages: 'I am a postgraduate in English, Political Science, and Urdu. I also give home tuition in these subjects now.' He was the only bookseller who communicated with me in English for the first half of the interview, which ran for almost two hours. However, as he felt more comfortable, he switched to Urdu and even recited a few ghazals[44] that he told me he had written.

Inside Mahila Haat, Khan's stall was not one of the well-curated stalls in Mahila Haat. After his personal collection sold out, he started selling what he could find from various sources, such as home libraries, schools, and some remainder stock from publishers. His initial stock (mostly his own collection) included books in Urdu, whereas now he sells a random selection of books in different languages, which includes anything from novels

---

[44] Ghazals are poetic compositions in Urdu and Persian characterised by couplets with a rhyme scheme and a recurring refrain, often expressing themes of love, loss, and longing.

and non-fiction to self-help, amongst other genres. As we saw in the previous section, a vendor's engagement with the available space on the footpath is an integral part of their day-to-day business, allowing them to attract customers in a certain way. Stall *sajana*, or arranging the stall, is a part of the specialisation that reflects their knowledge of how they can attract customers and how the readers may want the books displayed. Khan accepts that he doesn't put much effort into curating or selling books, which could be one of the reasons why few buyers visit his stall. Peculiarly, Khan was rather disappointed with the poor engagement with Urdu that the visitors of Daryaganj have come to exhibit over the years. 'You see, Urdu is not spoken commonly, especially with the new genera-tion, and it is not used as an official language as much as it was earlier. This is reflected in the [poor] sale and resale value of books in Urdu.' The fact that he cannot sell books in the language he is fond of may be one reason for the sense of detachment he feels vis-à-vis book vending. His disappointment extends further: 'People are overjoyed when someone uses an Urdu word or recites a couplet in Urdu. Yet, they do not want to learn the language.'

While Khan had a thorough knowledge of how this trade functions – he explained to me how the books had been sourced into this market over the years and who the key booksellers are – he did not find joy in selling books (compared to how, say, Rajesh Ojha or A. L. Verma enjoyed bookselling) – yet, he continues to do this despite only barely managing to make enough profit to run his house. His children are 'settled' and don't need his money – one of the reasons why he can continue. Khan's family doesn't support his business of selling books at the Sunday Patri Kitab Bazaar since he is not earning anything from this trade, and it demands much physical labour, which seems difficult for someone his of age to manage. But since he still has many books in stock, he feels the need to continue until he sells them. He seemed unconvinced by the option of selling the lot to the booksellers here or to a paper merchant. He likes to come to the market, he said, since it has become a part of his routine. Hence, bookselling becomes a habit, and not *shauq*. He questioned his attachment to the trade since he could not engage with it as he wanted to, because he was unable to sell Urdu books, the stock with which he started. 'Bookselling is an art', he exclaimed, 'and I am not good at this art'.

Another such 'detached' vendor worth mentioning here is Manmohan Singh. Book vending is not his only profession, as is common for a few booksellers at the bazaar.[45] He does iron-welding in a shop near where he lives in Jamnapar, East Delhi. He started out doing odd jobs such as embroidery on clothes and maintenance. He shares his stock of books with his friends at the Patri Kitab Bazaar. His only engagement is to sell the books and not worry about acquiring more stock or curating his stall. I asked him why his friends were helping him without taking a share of the profits. He told me he doesn't live with his family, is unmarried, and relies on his friends' support. I asked him why he was not married – all the booksellers I had interviewed had a family to support, mostly with the help of this business. '*Sach bataun, to koi mila hi nahin*': he couldn't find anyone, he said. Singh's case was unusual for me since several booksellers at Daryaganj Patri Kitab Bazaar entered the business with the help of a family member or, further, had some members of their family involved in the trade. In fact, the idea of kinship is typically associated with both large- and small-scale businesses in India. Singh, on the other hand, has found a community amidst the booksellers.

Interestingly, Singh is the only Sikh vendor I saw at the Patri Kitab Bazaar. He spoke to me in Punjabi once he realised I could speak it too. He felt more comfortable using his mother tongue and opened up to me about his life as a bookseller and otherwise – something that he doesn't get to do with other vendors or most of his customers. He doesn't have any books to sell in Punjabi, either. He would have liked to pursue that, he says, since he also reads Punjabi books and has an interest in the language. However, while Khan was unable to sell Urdu books despite the presence of Urdu in

---

[45] Watch vendor Uma Shankar Mishra's story here, where he informs us that his 'part-time' business of bookselling (since he only sells books on Sundays) earns him more money than his full-time employment as a helper at an air conditioning spare parts store (at his day job he manages Rs. 700–900 per day from a twelve-hour shift for five days a week, as against at least Rs. 4,000 per Sunday): www.facebook.com/AsiaFeatured/videos/1245210952356581.

the bazaar (unlike Chaudhry, who has established a network of buyers in the bazaar), books in Punjabi do not usually circulate as a part of the communication circuit that runs in Daryaganj Patri Kitab Bazaar. He did not seem very keen on this business, nor did he invest much capital or thought into it. He comes there to sell books among the community that he has gradually developed an attachment to, and that's about it. If not for his sense of belonging with other vendors, Singh might as well have also sold any other commodity.

2.4 Community, Growth, Resilience

There are formal and informal ways to identify the community of vendors at the Patri Kitab Bazaar. The formal ways include a written intimation of business to the civic authorities and registering oneself as a street vendor, so that one can comply with state and central policies such as the Street Vending (Protection of Livelihood and Regulation of Street Vending) Act, 2014. This Act protects the rights of urban street vendors and provides regulations for street vending activities. The vendors must safeguard these proofs of their registration. Apart from the *gulabi parchi* – a pink tax receipt provided by the MCD – and registration documents from before the relocation, vendors now retain proof of the bazaar's relocation to Mahila Haat, such as rent receipts received by individual vendors and the renewed *pakka* (proper) contract signed with the NrDMC that allows the vendors to stay at the Haat for three consecutive years.

Most vendors have been perpetually insecure about occupying the streets. Hence, to pre-empt any claims of illegality, they save all documents that carry a semblance of officiality. They have preserved the documents they were provided with when the Association was formed and the seemingly ephemeral *gulabi parchi*. These documents may also carry sentimental value. For instance, one of the vendors, showing me an old *gulabi parchi*, said he brings it to show it to the customers who ask him about his journey as a patri book vendor. Another bookseller declared his romantic association with this receipt: 'it is a relic – *yeh toh ek nishani hai*; how else will I and my grandchildren remember that I sold books here?' Even an ephemeral document such as the *gulabi parchi* reminds them of their presence in a transitory bazaar. The official documents, then, provide written recognition of a vendor's attachment to the place where they carried out their profession.

These documents show a vendor's official timeline at the *patri*. Whenever they are asked to verify or even describe their association with the bazaar, whether by the civic authorities or by keen photojournalists and ethnographers of the bazaar, these documents become a convenient way of declaring such attachment. For instance, it was common for a vendor to show me one of these documents while describing their life at the Patri Kitab Bazaar. Qamar Saeed – the King of Daryaganj, according to Wali, and one of the oldest booksellers at the bazaar – showed me a certificate of his registration as a street hawker at the Patri Kitab Bazaar, highlighting the date on which he registered, saying that that date was when he became sure that this was going to be his way of life. He was eighteen. He has spent forty years at the bazaar, serving as President of the Association of book vendors at Daryaganj. Most vendors keep photocopies of various documents that are meant to validate their presence on the streets only for one day. They also have these documents laminated because they realise that they might be required to, or may wish to, reproduce them in the future, even if they have only nostalgic significance. One bookseller said that he still has his *gulabi parchi* from before the official registration of the bazaar under the semi-regular *tehbazaari* system, from the 1982 Asiad Games (a day of significance for Delhi residents), confusing it with the Olympics: '*Mere paas bayasi ki parchi hai, jab Olympic khel hua tha. Main panni mein lagakar aaunga*' ('I will cover it with polythene and bring it for you'); '*Mera poora naam likha hua hai*' ('It has my "full name"').

Official documents, then, go beyond their bureaucratic function and serve as 'paper truths' or 'memory props'.[46] While these documents neither provide a full picture nor represent the event in its totality, their diversity results in a fuller, richer portrait of the elements at play. The *parchis* and official papers may not be the right proof, but they validate the vendor's role

---

[46] Stephen Legg (2008), *Spaces of Colonialism: Delhi's Urban Governmentalities* (John Wiley & Sons, 2008)

in the history and the present of the bazaar. Here, each retrospective document that the vendors produced has the added function of creating a biography of a bazaar that has, so far, remained undocumented, and which also obviously lacks a permanent architecture or infrastructure. The papers and *parchis* thus become a part of this absent architecture. The vendors did not share a tense relationship with the authorities until the relocation in September 2019. After the displacement, as discussed in detail in the previous section, these documents became a way for the vendors to mark their presence on the footpaths.

However, these documents are not entirely reliable in determining who is 'officially' a vendor at the Patri Kitab Bazaar. Suvrata Chowdhary, in his systematic study of the local weekly markets (LWMs) in Delhi, has the following to say about how an official database is *supposed to* be maintained by the MCD officials that accounts the numeration and other details about the vendors:

> The Municipal Corporation of Delhi does not distinguish between weekly markets and individual street vendors and hawkers. There is a provision in the Scheme[47] which states that a centralised database of the registrations of traders and vendors has to be maintained and full details like name, address, photograph etc., along with their locations. The information would be accessible in all Zones to avoid deli-cacy. A public notice inviting applications from squatters/ hawkers who are squatting/hawking without authorisation in MCD's jurisdiction and from unemployed persons who are desiring to make their livelihood by squatting/vending in accordance with the eligibility conditions would be adver-tised by the Central Licensing and Enforcement Cell, MCD in leading newspapers and shall also be displayed on the MCD website. The aforementioned provision of the scheme has only written importance. The MCD does not maintain

---

[47] Released in 2009, this scheme was later formulated into the Street Vendors (Protection of Livelihood) Act, 2014.

a systematic record of registered vendors, let alone of prospective applicants.[48]

Chowdhary's remarks on the inconsistencies in the official system that records the number, types, and degree of formality of street vendors, especially those in the local weekly markets, reflect the ambiguities found in Daryaganj Patri Kitab Bazaar. The official list of vendors generated as an appendix to officiate the 'Darya Ganj Patri Sunday Book Bazaar Welfare Association' under the Societies Registration Act of XXI of 1860 includes 258 names, with their names, dates of birth, address, and contact details. Each vendor also has a certificate authorising them to set up a stall on the designated pavements at Daryaganj. However, there were never as many vendors sitting on the *patri* at once, on any Sunday – only approximately 100. This was because some vendors, although registered individually, belong to a family that runs their stalls together. In this way, members of one family can set up extended stalls beyond the officially sanctioned space of six feet by four feet. By registering multiple family members, it was also easy for one person to replace another in case of a medical emergency or for other reasons. No official regular record was maintained regarding which vendor was present on which days. That is, while there are formal means to define and regulate this community of vendors, the vendors have found ways to escape the officiality.

Traditional vendors have kept the bazaar running for years by building a reliable knowledge corpora and showing resilience. Until several hundred other booksellers could join them and find stability, this continued to shape the bazaar. However, for both new and traditional vendors, what does it mean to 'grow' in this business? Firstly, there are newer ways of selling books because stocks and buyers' demands keep changing. Secondly, the way informal business is conducted keeps changing. For instance, regula-tions are updated by the civic authorities every few years. Also, vendors have continued to invent new ways of bookselling – for example, inside Mahila Haat, to match the new venue, new buyers, or new demands. Vendors updated their stock and adjusted the prices of books to compensate

[48] Chowdhary, 26.

for the loss during protests/periods of no sale when the street bazaar was shut down. Or, there is the creation of a new circuit: for instance, the study-material circuit branched out of the traditional circuit when vendors recognised a steady demand for both syllabus and out-of-syllabus books amongst the growing migrant student population in Delhi. For the traditional, old vendors, their previous knowledge helped them. For new vendors, this was a space for experimentation. In this way, it was easiest for the 'D' books vendors to adjust in the new space since they didn't have to update their stock – their stock and profit margins are decided by intermediaries who are not present at the bazaar. Some traditional vendors told me they were now inclined to sell 'D' books, given that the profit margin is guaranteed (to compensate for the losses they had incurred).

At the Patri Kitab Bazaar, the traditional vendors have relied on both vertical bonds of kinship and horizontal bonds of friendship to form a dense locality-specific social network. The rhetoric of *garv*, *shauq*, and *lagaav* was also clear in the narratives of vendors not selling at the Patri Kitab Bazaar but elsewhere. These are the vendors who, after selling books at the bazaar for a considerable period, either moved elsewhere or modified the scale of their business (i.e., moving away from this *patri* to another *patri*, a formal bookshop, or some other business related to books). *Patri* bazaar, particularly for *shauqeen* vendors, engenders a strong sense of community that remains even after they move away.

One such example is that of Om Mago, the owner of Om Books International. He was one of the first vendors to set up a stall for used books in Daryaganj. I was told by the other vendors that I must contact him if I wanted a 'complete' history of Daryaganj: '*Wo hi apko sab bata payenge. Wo shuru se yahaan the*' ('He will be able to tell you everything. He has been here since the beginning [of the market]'). And it was true: Mago narrated the history of Daryaganj Patri Kitab Bazaar, providing details of what it looked like, who the first vendors were, what kinds of books they sold, and how the business operated and flourished. While Mago's business has upscaled to international territories and he has entirely moved away from used titles and the Patri Kitab Bazaar, he tells me that he learned the ways of book business because of the connections he had built during his time as a vendor on the streets of Daryaganj. Such vendors are 'traditional vendors' of the bazaar, irrespective of their move, as they have played a significant role in this community's resilience.

However, given this strong sense of community, the traditional vendors have also created informal ways of exclusion: deciding who should be a part of the community and who must not be identified as one of their own. Such exclusion, or 'boundary work', is rhetorical and implies various practices of self-differentiation, wherein some members of a professional community will claim to be more authentic than others.[49] In the case of the vendors of the Patri Kitab Bazaar, there are two ways in which such a boundary has been created: female vendors of books, and vendors who sell 'D' books.

2.5 Boundary Work: The 'Non-Vendors'

2.5.1 Two Female Book Vendors: Asha and Vinita

Of the 258 vendors mentioned in the official list, only 8 are women. These women visited the market only in lieu of their husbands, sons, or fathers-in-law, except for Asha and Vinita.[50] Both Asha and Vinita were present regularly at their respective stalls. Asha's stall sold used books, and Vinita's sold out-of-syllabus children's books, such as books on the alphabet, simple mathematics, colouring books, and so on. Thus, both their stocks of books belonged to two major circuits that operated in the bazaar. How they did the business (or performed the role of a bookseller) – setting up the stalls and negotiating with the buyers each Sunday, and even taking major and minor business decisions – was no different than for any other regular, male seller at the Patri Kitab Bazaar. Asha was, in fact, an elected member of the now-dismantled Darya Ganj Patri Sunday Book Bazaar Welfare Association and held the position of treasurer. Likely, she was

---

[49] Thomas F. Gieryn, 'Boundary-Work and the Demarcation of Science from Non-Science', *American Sociological Review*, 48 (1983), 781–795.

[50] Kanupriya Dhingra, forthcoming book chapter in an edited volume (*Gender and the Book Trades*, ed. Elise Watson and Jessica Farrell-Jobst; https://brill.com/edcollbook/title/70509?language=en). It will focus on such on 'boundary work', discussing the 'housewifization' of women as 'inauthentic' members of the community of vendors at Daryaganj Sunday Book Bazaar.

merely a cursory representative of her gender, as mandated by the by-laws of the association. However, despite their visibly active role, their identity as vendors was not 'authorised' by the male vendors.

Since the very first Sunday of my fieldwork and throughout the protests held by the vendors between July and September 2019, and even after the relocation, I met Asha Devi every Sunday, and we often chatted more about the book market's situation than her life as a bookseller. A woman in her late fifties, she preferred staying in one place and not moving around the stall or the streets; she blamed her age for her aching back and knees. Asha expressed her refusal to identify herself as a bookseller as such; each time she would talk about her engagement with the market, she repeated this sentence: '*Ye aadmi logon ke hi bas ka kaam hai. Itni bhaari-bhaari kitabein auratein kaise uthyengi, aap hi batao?*' ('This business can only be run by men. How do you think women will manage handling such heavy stocks of books?'). Since her husband passed away, she has spent several years manning the bookstall, while her son Shekhar took their book business beyond the streets of Daryaganj: Shekhar dealt with the intermediaries and outsourced the stock of second-hand books to other countries. At the stall, Asha negotiated with the customers who visited the stall since Shekhar was rarely present at the site of business. Yet, instead of Asha, Shekhar was the one whom the rest of the booksellers engaged with: from informal discussions over *chai* about the business to buying books from him to sell on their stalls. He is one of the younger vendors but is known among the booksellers as someone who has gained extensive knowledge about the business. Since Asha (and Shekhar) sold second-hand English novels, they were both what I understand as traditional vendors of the Patri Kitab Bazaar. Yet, Shekhar was publicly acknowledged as one by the booksellers, but not Asha.

When I met Vinita Wadhwa, who was in her early forties, she was grieving for her husband, who had died in May 2019: 'He had a heart attack on a Sunday evening, after having spent the day on the *patri*, selling books.' When I met her in July 2019 at the *patri* and later inside Mahila Haat, her son Dev had just started to assist her and was quickly learning the tricks of the trade in order to take over whenever it was suitable. Vinita felt the need to find other means of employment because she couldn't identify herself as a bookseller. As in the case of Asha and Shekhar, other vendors would often communicate only with Dev rather than with Vinita about issues and opportunities related to the Patri Bazaar – say, issues related to the relocation or new stock coming in. Since Dev is younger and much less experienced than Shekhar, the vendors took it upon themselves to train him as a forthcoming vendor from the new generation, but one who would sell books at the bazaar in the traditional sense – what books to gather, building contacts that may be relevant for his business, how to negotiate with the customer and the intermediaries, and so on.

However, Vinita seemed familiar with the tricks of the trade when I met her. At their stall, they sold newly acquired out-of-syllabus supplementary course material for children, such as colouring books, books on alphabets and numbers, and some comics. Her husband's old assistant was responsible for selling the stock of old novels he had accumulated. In this sense, Vinita had created her own specialised stall. While Dev was still learning, she already knew what would sell and how to fetch profits. Vinita had taken over the business overnight since there was no other way to earn a livelihood. The family lived in a rented house, and the book business paid all their bills. Vinita was active during the protests that were held in July–September 2019, demonstrating her resilience by fighting for the streets and getting back to business, but, a few weeks after the NrDMC made the relocation official, she decided to move to Mahila Haat. She told me that she had to find some way to feed her family of two. While she waited for Dev to take over the business gradually, she looked for a more 'stable' job, since the book trade within Mahila Haat had been quite erratic. She was an active seller, much like Asha or any other male vendor. However, the two months when the Patri Kitab Bazaar was lifted off the streets had demotivated her due to the lack of stability in the book business at Mahila Haat. Trusting her skills as a businesswoman, she decided to sell homemade chocolates as a side business. This would also limit her interactions in a male-dominated space and wouldn't require her to depend on men who, apparently, ran the book business. However, since her experience and acquired training and knowledge were in bookselling, and that too in a bazaar-like space, she realised she couldn't easily apply it to another commodity. (This, in turn, testifies that this space and this commodity are specialised and require specific modes of training and the execution of that training in the business.) Learning how to sell chocolates – or, in other words, becoming a chocolate vendor – demanded a different skill and knowledge set. Eventually, Dev and Vinita decided to move their bookstall to a more permanent and 'proper' space for books, such as the North Campus of Delhi University, where the demand and circulation processes are more systematic and stable.

In a very conventional sense, Asha's and Vinita's cases are examples of the devaluation of work that women do outside the home. Asha Devi and Vinita are the only female vendors who ran independent bookstalls in the Patri Kitab Bazaar – both because their husbands had passed away and their sons could not stay at the stall regularly. Yet, both considered themselves merely 'assisting' with the bookselling business, and viewed the business as unsafe for women vis-à-vis procurement and sales in a visible male space. Vinita's father-in-law and other male booksellers would visit their stall every Sunday to check if they were safe and comfortable. The crowded streets of Old Delhi were home to a heterogeneous crowd prone to theft and petty crimes. The larger part of the vendors were men. Managing stocks of books from the godowns to their stall involved other men: rickshaw pullers and other labourers. Even while they actively engaged in the profession of selling books, Asha and Vinita see themselves as belonging to the space of the house and not the outside world of street vending – it was only out of necessity, and only until Dev could take over, that Vinita was willing to work. Even Asha expressed that this was one way for her to 'pass' her time, and nothing beyond that. In a way, this restriction is also cultural, whereby women are constrained by the boundaries of housework and not worldly affairs such as running a business. Consider Kiran's case. Kiran is a thirty-five-year-old woman whose husband is a heart patient. He used to sell books near the Delite Cinema, but since 2018, around the time it became difficult for them to manage their finances, Kiran replaced her husband as a vendor. Her husband is not happy that she 'goes outside the house to work' – '*main bahar kaam karti hoon, unhein achha nahin lagta*', she says. He would rather she stayed inside.

Daryaganj Patri Kitab Bazaar is visibly a male-dominated space, professionally and socially. The only two regular female vendors could never associate themselves with the space. It is, however, common to see women vending on the streets across Delhi. For instance, at a rather famous street market in Central Delhi, popularly known as Janpath Gujarati Market, it is mostly women who sell Gujarati artefacts, jewellery, upholstery, and bags. However, the adjacent imported clothes market is also populated by male vendors. Janpath Gujarati Market is set in a different lane, and is an exclusive space for women to sell their goods around familiar people. Daryaganj Patri Kitab Bazaar is larger in size and scale and is situated in a more conservative part of the city. Hence, even if it is not obviously stated that the space is unsafe for women or is exclusively male-dominated, this is assumed, and it shows. The civic authorities speculated and argued that the bounded architecture and outlook of Mahila Haat would be a 'safer' space for women to pursue book vending. There were certainly more female members/vendors seen inside the Haat, but most were sitting with their husbands, brothers, or other male family members. One of the reasons for an increase in this number was also that the vendors needed extra help in setting up their stalls inside the new site. Since it was already an expensive arrangement compared to the streets, family members, especially women, became suitable unpaid labour. However, it would be premature to claim that the conventional boundary that the vendors have created will loosen with the change in space.

Meenu and her daughter Divya are also worth mentioning here. Both are members of the extended Aggarwal family, as is Vinita. Meenu and Divya began coming to the market to participate in the protest. During the protest, Divya mentioned that due to a family feud the Aggarwal brothers were fighting for their individual stalls and not as a unit, which is why both mother and daughter had come to support her father. Divya worked in the sales department of a jewellery shop and had to leave the protest site for work every Sunday. Her mother was present throughout the protests. Both Meenu and Divya are registered in the official list of vendors. However, while they were not authentic members of this community because of their irregular participation in the bazaar's day-to-day, Divya and Meenu were still expected to participate in the protests.

It was challenging for female booksellers to establish their ownership of the bazaar space – they lacked the pride or pleasure to openly claim it.

According to them, they don't 'fit in'. The organisation of the vendor community at the Patri Kitab Bazaar shows a persistence of older family forms and structures within which individuals, particularly women, must continue to operate. The female vendors at the bazaar accommodate their agency and autonomy within the existing constraints of duty and obligations, both social and familial.[51] Asha and Vinita are not creating any new forms of specialisation or adding to the knowledge corpus. Instead, they choose to act within the traditional norms the male vendors have created and continue to create. In this view, if I were to disregard how the male vendors view them or how they choose to express their rhetoric of belonging, instead of seeing them as 'non-vendors', I would rather place them with other 'detached vendors' such as A. R. Khan and Manmohan Singh. Female vendors at the bazaar have not (yet) been able to form their independent identity as proper vendors of Daryaganj Patri Kitab Bazaar.

However, gender was not the only means of bias. To reaffirm what makes a vendor part of the traditional community of vendors, the type of books that they sell played a key role. This is where the vendors of 'D' books were dissociated from the traditional community and were placed outside the implicit boundary.

2.5.2 Vendors of 'D *ki kitab*'

During the 2019 protests, K. R. Khanna boisterously described himself as the 'father of this market' each time I or any media personnel interviewed him – a claim other booksellers were keen to discredit. They claimed that other older members, such as Om Mago or Sushil Kumar, had started the market. Nevertheless, whether or not he was the father of the market, he did sell books at the bazaar for a long time. Khanna gave up his allotted space on Netaji Subhash Marg some time ago and now helps his son, who runs a shop in Kamla Nagar, Delhi-07. Referring to himself as a paternal figure of authority, or a *buzurg* (elderly member of a community), was his way of reclaiming his share in the social memory of the community's past and present.

---

[51] Srivastava, *Passionate Modernity*, p. 274.

Why am I discussing Khanna ji here? He introduced me to the term 'D' books, which is what the vendors call pirated or digitally produced books. He then played a pivotal role in introducing me to another aspect of bookselling at the bazaar: the boundary the booksellers create by excluding the vendors of 'D' books as authentic members of the community of vendors at Daryaganj.

Khanna exclaimed on behalf of what he understands as the authentic community of vendors: '*Humne is patri ko sincha hai, hum ise kharab nahin hone denge*' ('We have nurtured this Patri; we will not let it deteriorate'). He addresses the authentic community of vendors at the Patri Kitab Bazaar as 'we'/'*hum*' while he 'others' the D-book vendors. For Khanna and several other vendors, the vendors of digitally pirated books are diminishing the value of the Patri Kitab Bazaar. The vendors of 'D' books are outside the shared rhetoric of *garv* and *lagaav* and are equated with 'other', ordinary street vendors and hawkers who should find a place elsewhere. This was a typical case of a community's resistance to change, with a gradual loss of traditional static bonds to social and spatial change.

The networks in which the vendors of pirated books are placed are distinct from the traditional networks with which older booksellers engage.[52] The notion of tradition is closely related to collective social memory, whereby beliefs and customs are handed down from generation to generation. Tradition is often linked to strong embeddedness and attachment to place and can frequently be found where a core group of stakeholder's generations have survived. Whenever I asked the vendors of non-pirated books about the processes of procurement and circulation of the books, most of them provided similar, overlapping narratives: surplus or imported stocks, institutional or private libraries, and so on. Having a shared network which runs each of their businesses highlighted that they have traced a tradition for their community. On the other hand, pirated books have their own 'communication circuit', which is outside the aforementioned tradition. These booksellers do not go through the conventional means of acquiring used books, such as publishers, libraries, auction sales,

---

[52] See Kanupriya Dhingra, 'The 'D-Books' of Daryaganj Sunday Book Market'. *Comparative Critical Studies* (2021), 309–326.

paper markets, and so on. Instead, they are connected to the printers directly. In this way, they become a more immediate part of the suggested parallel communication circuit, having only a few actors within the circuit to communicate with. There is something worth noting here vis-à-vis the 'newness' of these books. Since D-Books are duplicates of the latest releases, they are indeed *nayi-jaisi*, unlike second-hand books or photocopied study-material. Hence, the knowledge corpus of D-book vendors is also unique and distinguishable from that of other vendors of the Patri Kitab Bazaar. Theirs is thus a community within a community, wherein most of these vendors are younger and new to the profession of bookselling, and only sell pirated books.

I met Rajiv almost every Sunday in 2019. He sold pirated books out of a Hyundai Santro car. It was interesting to see that instead of the temporary space of the street, he chose the temporary space of a car to sell his 'new' books – pirated copies of the latest releases. Rajiv greeted me every day and discussed the latest issues with the space of the market, especially how the MCD was creating problems for vendors of the *patri*. Contrary to what Khanna told me, he seemed to share a good bond with other regular vendors as well – that is, he was not seen as a 'threat', which is the idea that Khanna endorsed. However, unlike vendors of second-hand books, who would often go in detail while explaining their 'communication circuit', Rajiv left most of my questions related to his business unanswered (questions such as how these books reach this book market, who are the major printers, are there any middlemen involved, is there a threat around the illegal procurement, production, or sale, and so on). '*Hum naye log hain, nayi kitabein bechte hain*', is all he would say – 'We are new vendors, we sell new books.' This was true for the rest of the vendors of pirated books as well. They were acutely aware of the dangers of sharing exhaustive information about their business, which is largely illegal, even if it is growing fast and brings in much profit for the sellers. Piracy has existed in the Daryaganj Sunday Patri Kitab Bazaar for decades. Having evolved newer formats of piracy and even newer ways of conducting business, the meta-community of vendors of pirated books are the ones to take the Patri Kitab Bazaar into the future. Their reluctance to share information also reflected their self-awareness of being on the periphery of the book business

in the Patri Kitab Bazaar, if not completely outside the traditional boundaries. That is, even as their business was proliferating on the *patri*, and the
patri was, in fact, a profitable site of business, they would rather discuss the
general manner of operation of the *patri* than distinguish their community as
a principal unit. This was untrue for the vendors of the other two circuits.

The sellers of pirated books do not undervalue their stock. Either they
convinced customers that their books were not pirated or they said that the
pirated books are, in fact, *behtar* ('better') than the original – they are
available much earlier than the used copies, and at a fixed price. So, no
'chik-chik' (haggling). Therefore, this became an additional burden for the
vendor of the traditional circuit, especially several such who sold novels to
the non-specialised reader not looking for 'rare' copies. In my interviews
with them, traditional vendors also defined their authenticity in terms of *not*
selling pirated books – the fact that they had to make this point out loud to
an ethnographer of the marketspace made their sense of incongruity with
the vendors of 'D' books more apparent. One of their common complaints
was that 'duplicate books are available across the city; they can sit anywhere
else'. Why, indeed, do these booksellers set up their stalls here? Is it simply
because this market receives a large number of book buyers?

Modern-day piracy is a result of the introduction of modern technology to
printing and publishing. As low-cost technologies of mechanical and digital
reproduction have become popular and accessible, it has become easier and
cheaper to produce 'D' books and sell them at the same price as a second-hand
copy, but with a higher profit margin. Even as pirated books have their own
production ecosystem, they do not have an independent ecosystem for
circulation. For that, there are ways in which the structure of a bazaar is
helpful to sustain this business. In addition, selling pirated books anywhere
else in the city's less crowded sites also entails higher visibility. This would
require the vendors to engage in complex networks of seeking permissions
from the civic authorities, which these vendors certainly want to avoid.

The resilience that any community retains is reflected in its capacity to
absorb disturbances and reorganise while undergoing changes, whilst
retaining the same structure, function, and identity. These members also
provide feedback. In the case of Patri Kitab Bazaar, D-book vendors do not
align with the traditional networks, nor do they bear any generational

connections. They are an 'addition' to this community in the ways in which they add to the bazaar's present-day (and possibly future) structure, function, and identity. Do the vendors of pirated books share the traditional community's resilience and attachment to the place? I witnessed an example of this resilience in the vendors of pirated books first-hand during the protests held between July and September 2019. Since the traditional community had divided itself into two groups – those who had decided to relocate and those who were against the decision – the reluctance displayed by the vendors of duplicate books to outgrow the outmoded space of the streets could be interpreted as their way of supporting the traditional community of vendors. At the outset of the protests, while the booksellers were trying to establish the validity of their claims to the limited street slots, the mainstream booksellers of Daryaganj regarded the vendors of pirated books as peripheral. This attitude underscored the low regard for their knowledge and background. Later, the same set of 'authentic'/traditional booksellers sought to partner with these other(ed) vendors to represent a majority for the relocation prompted by the civic authorities.[53] Most of the vendors of pirated books decided to stay on the streets for a good span of time – possibly because the streets were more likely than Mahila Haat to accommodate their 'grey-area' business and because they had fostered a sense of operating their business on the streets.

In conclusion, at the Patri Kitab Bazaar, the *habitus* of the vendors, their education, training, social background, circumstances, family, and so forth, all come into play as they indulge in precarious modes of self-management. By way of their situated knowledge, the vendors give the Patri Kitab Bazaar its unique identity. Over time, the vendors acquire the capacity to relate and negotiate with traditional forms that are declining or being reworked in the bazaar according to new logic. Within these emerging mechanisms, such as those the vendors of 'D' books bring in, the traditional vendors are no longer the privileged mediators. Instead, they must find ways to foster new, emerging networks.

---

[53] Around the first week of September 2019, when Mahila Haat was given as an option to the book vendors, the 'D'-book vendors joined 'traditional'/vendors of used books who still wanted to sell books on the pavement.

2.6 Reflection: Who are the Vendors at Daryaganj
Patri Kitab Ba*ʒ*aar?

They can be a Dilliwallah or a migrant who aspires to be a Dilliwallah. Some may have been, currently are, or may choose in the future to become proper booksellers. This is why booksellers come here to gain knowledge about bookselling, and why some deploy existing knowledge about books. All in all, even as their knowledge, purpose, and degree of investment varies, they are all informed street vendors with specialised knowledge of sourcing books and selling them on the street.

What sets the Patri Kitab Bazaar vendors apart from other regular street vendors? These vendors like to differentiate themselves from your regular *chaiwallah* and vendors of imported clothes at the Sarojini Nagar market. Even though they are a part of the informal sector, they do not equate that with any sense of inferiority. This is because specialising requires time and knowledge about resourcing and the value of the commodity. Specialisation, in the case of the Patri Kitab Bazaar vendors, means acquiring the necessary knowledge corpus, but also focusing on only one circuit. From the vendor's point of view, it is quite organised, not only because of history or officialdom, even as they enter this profession by chance. Here, the commodity in question is also eclectic – each second-hand book is, in a way, unique. How does Puneet Kumar know that 'competition books' will find repeated 'high-quality' buyers at the bazaar? Must A. R. Khan remain disappointed that Urdu books don't sell at the bazaar and not change his stock? S. Chaudhry comes to the bazaar precisely because he has found a market for his Urdu publications! Why does Swastik Dogra not sell the more familiar stock of spiritual books? How does Manish Kumar know what *really* qualifies as a rare book? Why does Bheem not worry about acknowledging this distinction when selling such books?

The knowledge of the booksellers is situated in the ways of the streets and in the books they sell. Qamar Saeed once told me '*Hum khud aathvi tak hi parhe hue hain. Angreʒi bolni nahin aati. Par humein itna experience hai ki kitab ki shakal saamne aate hi hum fauran samajh jaate hain ki yeh kitab kis publisher ki ya kis writer ki hai, aur iski kya value hai*' ('I only studied till the eighth grade. I cannot speak in English. But I have enough experience that the moment I see a book, I can gauge who has published the book, who their author is, and the precise value of a book'). Their 'knowledge corpora' is shaped by knowledge of informal street business as well as knowledge about books. The latter is equally, if not more, informed by the materiality of books. A bookseller doesn't have to read the books or know about the authors and publishers (though it is good if they do because it helps them judge the value of books in a better manner). Rather, unlike in a bookshop, a bookseller here can sustain their business without this knowledge. Instead, they require parallel knowledge: being familiar with what type of genre sells, how old a book might be, how much marginalia is enough marginalia, that books can be sold without covers, in duplicate and photocopied formats, and so on. Their knowledge about Delhi's reading public is parallel too – they need to know who occupies Delhi's streets (i.e., the 'accidental' reader). In other words, their business runs because of these parallel readers who seek inexpensive books and those who seek rare books, and this is reflected in the vendors' degree of investment. Hence, in the case of vendors of Daryaganj, their training is achieved through their experience on the streets, their knowledge of this profession, their knowledge from their previous professions, and knowledge that previous vendors have created and continue to form.

Depending on when they arrive in the bazaar, the booksellers survey their sources, and through a mix of chance encounters and repeated efforts, they accumulate knowledge. This knowledge enables them to generate value, make profits, and sustain their livelihoods – that is, their 'forms of knowing and doing.'[54] The sellers' knowledge corpora is neither entirely a result of free will nor determined by structures, but created by an interplay between the two over time. The practices and processes at the bazaar are not reproduced unconsciously. With time, and over a prolonged period of recurrence and repetition, the sellers use their existing skills and bring nuance into their behaviour and knowledge, combined with their interest, *lagaav*, and *shauq*. A totality of their experience, skills, attachment, and *shauq* shapes how the bazaar functions. Then there are those who could not, chose not to, or were

<hr />

[54] Gago.

not allowed to continue to sell books here. The traditional community of vendors plays a significant role in defining its membership and boundaries.

In this section, 'locating' the vendors meant marking their arrival and examining their presence in the bazaar. We saw that even though chance or happenstance has a huge role to play in how the booksellers arrive at the bazaar or in their search for books for their stalls and in how they establish their clientele, there have been other conditions that influenced whether they decide to turn to bookselling at Daryaganj: unemployment, lack of stability in the previous business, migration, because of their family or community, education or previous training wherein some booksellers have been involved in bookselling beforehand or were trained into it by their 'predecessors' in the bazaar. As vendors of second-hand and duplicate books who found their way to the bazaar in the way that they did, in creating unique knowledge, by establishing a unique relationship with the space and the commodity that they sell, and then in deciding the professional and social boundaries for their community, the vendors of Daryaganj Patri Kitab Bazaar can be seen as 'parallel' to what is understood as a proper bookseller.

Epilogue: 'Joy' as a Method

Why must I record the story of Daryaganj and its booksellers? First, to reconstruct the history of Daryaganj Patri Kitab Bazaar and examine its ethnographic present. The trajectories of the vendors form an integral part of the totality of this history and help create a richer portrait of the elements at play. The individual accounts I rely on are as much a part of the 'official memory', serving as archives of knowledge previously considered naïve or insufficiently conceptual.

Second, this project belongs to the dialogic discipline of book history, which deals with a history of documents and the personnel associated with production, transmission, and reception processes. In most cases, the archives that any book historian relies on are transient and ephemeral. For this project, the space of the bazaar itself possesses a transitory character. The bazaar is not a permanent establishment, but is only available at certain intervals. It has run a continued risk of complete erasure/disappearance. There is a lack of adequately reliable and comprehensive written accounts about this market's history and evolution over at least six decades. Hence, the narratives that come into view through the booksellers contribute to the construction of a people's history of the Patri Kitab Bazaar and define how the 'everyday' – or, rather, every Sunday – shapes up here. Hence, to record such a space or to study the space of Daryaganj Patri Bazar as an archive, I turn to what seems to be one of the most reliable methodological tools: the memory of the people who made this space and the narrative they chose to provide. By way of their participation, they have come to represent this book market. Their personal histories, once integrated, form a collective biography of Daryaganj Sunday Patri Kitab Bazar, and that is what they share. That is, the story of the vendors becomes the story of the bazaar.

With the help of ethnography and oral interviews, I was able produce a biography of a bazaar by situating (or 'locating') myself in the field – I took notes, photographs, and time-lapse videos to study the rhythms of the bazaar and later transcribed the narratives I had elicited. The vendors at Daryaganj were eager to share their stories. They shared with me their *lagaav* – for them, the Daryaganj Patri Kitab Bazaar went beyond just being a business. Every initial interaction with a bookseller, without fail, led to a prolonged conversation. While discussing the vendors, I show how the sellers find *'enjoy'* (enjoyment) and *maza* (fun) while selecting books for their stalls. In my own transition from being an ordinary buyer to being a *shauqeen* buyer and ethnographer, and then to being an active supporter and part of the community, what gave me *joy* was the ability to translate my theories into action beyond the academy – due to the relocation, I unexpectedly became part of a larger movement of protecting the bazaar and retaining the space of the street. Knowing about my visibility as an English-speaking researcher from the UK, the sellers often chose to convey their demands through me (among other similar figures associated with the bazaar in various capacities). I became a part of this 'community of memory', as it were. Hence, this shared rhetoric of *joy* progressively became part of my methodology and helped me stay curious about the space and find new ways to perform book history. While the struggles of the vendors and the fragility of the space were in front of my eyes, the ability of the bazaar to enable joy and promote *lagaav* seemed to me a crucial part of its affective power. By foregrounding affect, I could propose a revised understanding of the bazaar and its *bazaaris*. 'Space' need not only be understood geometrically – it is closely related to emotions and feelings, including resilience, nostalgia, and joy.

Select Bibliography

Bhattacharya, Bhaswati (2018). 'Adda and Public Spaces of Sociability before the ICH', in *Much Ado over Coffee: Indian Coffee House Then and Now*. London: Routledge.

Bhattacharya, Diti (2024). *Unfolding Spatial Movements in the Second-Hand Book Market in Kolkata: Notes on the Margins in the Boipara*. New York: Routledge.

Certeau, Michel de (1984). *The Practice of Everyday Life*. Berkeley: University of California Press.

Chatterjee, Rimi B. (2006). *Empires of the Mind: A History of the Oxford University Press in India Under the Raj*. New Delhi: Oxford University Press.

Chowdhary, Suvrata (2017). The Local Weekly Markets of Delhi: Operating in the Formal 'Space' and Informal Economy. *E-journal of the Indian Sociological Society*, 1 (2), 3–31.

Darnton, Robert (1982). What Is the History of Books? *Daedalus*, 111 (3), 65–83.

Dhingra, Kanupriya (2019). Will Delhi Soon Have a Daryaganj-Used-Books-Market-Shaped Hole? *Scroll.in*. https://scroll.in/author/17473.

Dhingra, Kanupriya (2019). Delhi's Daryaganj Book Bazaar Has a New, Sanitised Home, Which Has Benefits as Well as Drawbacks. *Scroll.in*. https://scroll.in/author/17473.

Dhingra, Kanupriya (2019). Delhi's Daryaganj Second-Hand Books Market: Going, Going ... but Not Quite Gone Yet? *Scroll.in*. https://scroll.in/author/17473.

Dhingra, Kanupriya (2020). Why the Lockdown and Physical Distancing Have All but Ended Delhi's Iconic Used Books Market. *Scroll.in*. https://scroll.in/author/17473.

Dhingra, Kanupriya (2020). The Death of a Book Bazaar – *Himal Southasian*. www.himalmag.com/comment/the-death-of-a-book-bazaar-daryaganj.

Dhingra, Kanupriya (2021). The 'D-Books' of Daryaganj Sunday Book Market. *Comparative Critical Studies*, 18 (2–3), 309–326.

Gago, Veronica (2018). What are Popular Economies? Some Reflections from Argentina. *Radical Philosophy*, 2 (02), 31–38. https://bit.ly/3RwQS6O.

Geertz, Clifford (1978). The Bazaar Economy: Information and Search in Peasant Marketing. *The American Economic Review*, 68 (2), 28–32.

Genette, Gerard (1997). *Paratexts: Thresholds of Interpretation*. Cambridge: Cambridge University Press.

Gieryn, Thomas F. (1983). Boundary-Work and the Demarcation of Science from Non-Science. *American Sociological Review*, 48 (6), 781–95.

Guha, Ramchandra (2018). Save the Daryaganj Book Bazaar, Once Again. *Hindustan Times*, 16 January.

Jamatia, Hamari (2011). Women Only: MCD's Mahila Haat to Open in April. *Indian Express*, 18 February.

Lefebvre, Henri (2004). *Rhythmanalysis: Space, Time and Everyday Life*. London: Continuum.

Legg, Stephen (2008). *Spaces of Colonialism: Delhi's Urban Governmentalities*. Chichester: John Wiley & Sons.

Massey, Doreen (2005). *For Space*. London: SAGE Publications.

Naim, Choudri Mohammed (2011). Syed Ahmad and his two books called 'Asar-al-Sanadid'. *Modern Asian Studies*, 45 (3), 669–708.

Sadana, Rashmi (2012). *English Heart, Hindi Heartland: The Political Life of Literature in India*. Ranikhet: Permanent Black.

Sadana, Rashmi (2018). 'We Are Visioning It': Aspirational Planning and the Material Landscapes of Delhi's Metro. *City & Society*, 30 (2), 186–209.

Soofi, Mayank Austen (2019). City Heritage: The History of Daryaganj's Sunday Book Bazaar, Central Delhi – *The Delhi Walla*. www.thedelhi

walla.com/2019/08/21/city-heritage-daryaganjs-sunday-book-bazaar-cen
tral-delhi/.

Srivastava, Sanjay (2007). *Passionate Modernity: Sexuality, Class, and Consumption in India*. New Delhi: Routledge.

Srivastava, Sanjay (2015). *Entangled Urbanism: Slum, Gated Community, and Shopping Mall in Delhi and Gurgaon*. New Delhi: Oxford University Press.

Sharma, Vibha (2017). Mahila Haat, Ramlila Ground may Host Weddings, Private Parties Soon. *Hindustan Times*, 20 January.

Acknowledgements

I am deeply thankful to Samantha Rayner and Eben Muse for the opportunity to publish my research in this exciting new format. I appreciate the anonymous reviewers for their positive feedback and constructive suggestions.

I owe a debt of gratitude to Francesca Orsini for supervising my doctoral thesis at SOAS, University of London, which forms the foundation of this Element. Her intellectual engagement at every stage of this project has shaped it for the better. Her continued mentorship has shown me new ways to be curious about books, book spaces, and the people who nurture them.

The Felix Trust and the Doctoral Fieldwork Award, SOAS, generously supported this work. The Summer Residency in Manuscript and Print Studies in June and July 2023 at the Institute of English Studies, School of Advanced Study, University of London, provided a conducive environment for further framing this research.

This Element is made out of fragments of many borrowed voices. My debt to the vendors of Daryaganj is too huge for a conventional thanks – I hope this Element does justice to their fascinating stories. I seek their forgiveness for any loss of quality and power when their words were transferred from the sound of the voice to the written page and from their varieties of Hindi, Punjabi, and Urdu to English. There was a significant period in 2019 when I feared the bazaar might disappear. Yet, the resilience of the booksellers remained a steady source of motivation for me. Qamar ji, A. L. Verma ji, Sumit ji, Asha ji, Manish ji, Surendra ji, Dilshad ji, and Sandeep ji – *aapke bharose aur protsahan ke liye shukriya*.

During my ethnography, I got the opportunity to meet a few exceptional *Dilliwallahs*. I am grateful to Daryaganj veterans Sohail Hashmi ji, Late Abdul Sattar ji, and B. N. Uniyal ji for sharing their *shauq* for Daryaganj's history, books, and people. They were my window to a period gone by, and it was enchanting to see these cataloguers of the city talk so passionately about it. Spending time with them was nothing short of an education.

Thanks to Abhijit Gupta and Sanjay Srivastava – their intellectual influence manifests in this work. I am grateful to Raisa Wickrematunge from *Himal SouthAsian* and Arunava Sinha from *Scroll* for giving me the chance to share significant news and narratives about the bazaar, particularly when it was going through a phase of uncertainty and needed attention from the general public. The audience feedback at various seminars, talks, and conferences has been exceptionally helpful for this project. I especially thank the British Library, the Bodleian Libraries Centre for the Study of the Book, and the SHARP community.

Madhav, thank you for being my anchor. To Uttaran and Sadaf, for sharing my *lagaav* for *Dilli*. To Punam, Sharmada, Raahi, Rani, Amber, and Ira, for their tireless emotional support. To Alfisha, for her editorial expertise and delightful friendship.

This Element is dedicated to my parents, Rashmi and Vijay Dhingra, and my brother Jiten. Your inexhaustible faith in my abilities continues to sustain me.

About the Author

Dr Kanupriya Dhingra researches the history of the book and print cultures, focusing on Delhi (India), from an ethnographic perspective. She is a Board of Directors member at the Society for the History of Authorship, Reading, and Publishing (SHARP). She teaches at the Jindal School of Languages and Literature, OP Jindal Global University.

Cambridge Elements ☰

Publishing and Book Culture

SERIES EDITOR
Samantha Rayner
University College London

Samantha Rayner is Professor of Publishing and Book Cultures
at UCL. She is also Director of UCL's Centre for Publishing,
co-Director of the Bloomsbury CHAPTER (Communication
History, Authorship, Publishing, Textual Editing and
Reading) and co-Chair of the Bookselling Research Network.

ASSOCIATE EDITOR
Leah Tether
University of Bristol

Leah Tether is Professor of Medieval Literature and Publishing
at the University of Bristol. With an academic background in
medieval French and English literature and a professional
background in trade publishing, Leah has combined her
expertise and developed an international research profile in
book and publishing history from manuscript to digital.

ABOUT THE SERIES

This series aims to fill the demand for easily accessible, quality texts available for teaching and research in the diverse and dynamic fields of Publishing and Book Culture. Rigorously researched and peer-reviewed Elements will be published under themes, or 'Gatherings'. These Elements should be the first check point for researchers or students working on that area of publishing and book trade history and practice: we hope that, situated so logically at Cambridge University Press, where academic publishing in the UK began, it will develop to create an unrivalled space where these histories and practices can be investigated and preserved.

Cambridge Elements ⹀

Publishing and Book Culture

Bookshops and Bookselling

Gathering Editor: Eben Muse
Eben Muse is Senior Lecturer in Digital Media at Bangor
University and co-Director of the Stephen Colclough Centre
for the History and Culture of the Book. He studies the impact
of digital technologies on the cultural and commercial space of
bookselling, and he is part-owner of a used bookstore in the
United States.

ELEMENTS IN THE GATHERING

Printed in the United States
by Baker & Taylor Publisher Services